IMAGES of BYZANTIUM

Learning about Icons

Stuart I. Robinson

IMAGES of BYZANTIUM

Learning about Icons

Stuart I Robinson

Loizou Publications
London

Loizou Publications

29, Doveridge Gardens, London, N13 5BJ

First Published 1996

Printed in Great Britain by Antony Rowe Ltd, Chippenham, Wiltshire.

I S B N 0 9521246 4 5

To the memory of Wolfgang Brehm.

CONTENTS

ACKNOWLEDGEMENTS

I am grateful to a number of people who so generously assisted with the creation of this publication. Sincere thanks are due to:

Loizos Loizou who, in the first instance, encouraged me to write the book.

Fr. Silouan of St. John the Baptist Orthodox Monastery, Tolleshunt Knights, who guided me in the direction of some of the essential literature.

David and Pat Packer who spent seemingly endless hours assisting with typing and layout.

Jennifer Speake who kindly read and commented upon the manuscript and whose suggestions for improvement were invaluable. A very special thanks.

Then there were family and friends who found time to assist with proof reading.

Gratitude is also due to the numerous institutions and individuals who kindly granted permission for the use of illustrative material.

Finally, I am greatly indebted to the genius of Master Iconographer, Dr. Guillem Ramos-Poqui, who taught me how to paint icons and who inspired me to learn as much about them as I could.

List of Illustrations

Black and White Plates: (Pages 27-38)

List of Diagrams *(Pages 39-42)*

All maps and diagrams by the author.

Sources of Illustrative Material

The Publisher would like to thank the following individuals and institutions for generously granting permission for the use of illustrative material.

1. Maria Andipa and Son Icon Gallery, Knightsbridge, London, England. (Plates 3, 4, 6, 7, 8 and 11)

2. Ekdotike Athenon SA., Athens, Greece. (Plate 9)

3. The Provost and Fellows of Eton College, Berkshire, England. (Plate 1)

4. Dr. Sophocles Sophocleous, Centre of Cultural Heritage, Nicosia, Cyprus. (Plate 5)

5. St. Vladimir's Seminary Press, New York, United States of America. (Plates 2, 10 and cover illustration)

FOREWORD

In recent years interest in the art of the Orthodox Church has burgeoned amongst the general public. Opportunities for easier travel in the Orthodox countries of eastern Europe and the wider exposure of Orthodox Christian art in galleries and publications in the West have combined to make increasing numbers of people in the non-Orthodox world aware of the particular power and beauty of icons - but aware also of their strangeness in relation to western conceptions of religious art. With their roots in ancient conventions that run back in many instances to the earliest Christian centuries, unaffected by the innovations of the Renaissance or by the personal whim of the artist, traditional icons carry a different - perhaps dauntingly different - charge from that of Western images of the same subject.

The difference between Eastern and Western Christendom in the ways that they describe the process of creation of a religious image is profoundly indicative of these wider differences. In the adherence to standard patterns, set out in handbooks that prescribe minutiae of form and colour, the icon painter is constrained, but also supported, by tradition in a way that is totally alien to most modern notions of artistic autonomy or individualism. The creator of icons is an iconographer, literally a writer of icons; such a writer is no more at liberty to alter a model at will than is a person copying an antique manuscript at liberty to add to or subtract from the original as undisciplined fancy suggests.

Images of Byzantium: Learning about Icons is a primer that will enable the non-Orthodox to begin to "read" the traditional Orthodox icon in all its doctrinal, devotional, historical and artistic contexts. The aesthetic appeal through which icons generally first attract the attention of an uncommitted onlooker of a different Christian denomination (or indeed of no Church at all) is thereby enriched through a deeper understanding of this unique art form that is so much more than merely an art form.
Stuart Robinson's own love of icons in all their aspects shines through the book.

Jennifer Speake

“Since the invisible One became visible by taking on flesh, you can fashion the image of Him whom you saw.

Since He who has neither body, nor form nor quantity nor quality, who goes beyond all grandeur by the excellence of His nature, He, being of Divine nature, took on the condition of a slave and reduced Himself to quantity and to quality by clothing Himself in human features.

Therefore, paint on wood and present for contemplation Him who desired to become visible”

St. John of Damascus

1

THE EVOLUTION OF THE ICON

Introduction

The word icon comes from the Greek word *eikon* which means image. Many of us recognise icons as beautiful paintings on a gold background depicting Christ, the Virgin Mary, the Saints and other subjects of a biblical nature. These paintings are mostly, but not exclusively, found in churches of Eastern Orthodox Christianity. Orthodox Christianity, although practised worldwide, is mainly centred on countries in the eastern part of Europe such as Greece, Serbia, Macedonia and, of course, Russia.
The evolution of the icon is the coming together of a number of cultures - especially Greek, Roman and Christian - and although it was a cornerstone of art during the era of the Byzantine Empire (330-1453 AD), it did have its beginnings much earlier than this.

As icons are religious paintings on a Christian theme, it may be a good idea to try to trace their origins from the beginning of the Christian Era.

The Early Christian Era

Although images of some sort have always played an important part in our lives, for the earliest Christians the idea of the image presented, at first, a significant problem because of its role, at the time, in pagan worship. The first Christians considered the image to be a form of idolatry. They would find it difficult, however, to develop their faith in isolation as they would soon be influenced by other cultures in the regions they inhabited. These influences were mainly from the pagan Greeks and Romans, both of whom believed that images possessed certain mystical qualities.

For these reasons the meeting places of the early Christians were not decorated with any types of image. In addition to this the communities were usually small and poor and could not afford to pay for such decoration. It was also important that as a persecuted minority they should keep a low profile and not do anything that would attract attention to themselves. Slowly, however, this attitude changed and in the decorations later to be found in the catacombs in Rome, we can detect the beginnings of a Christian art. These catacombs were underground tombs where the people went to pay their respects to the dead and it is here that we first see scenes from the Old Testament appearing. What the Christians were now starting to do was to take certain pagan images and give them their own, different and deeper, meaning. It now became acceptable, therefore, to decorate places of worship with scenes which were also designed to serve as a method of teaching new followers about the Christian faith. Besides using pagan symbols with new meanings, they also created new symbols of their own. By the end of the second century, therefore, symbols of particular inspiration to the Christians began to appear.

During excavations of a site at Dura-Europos - a town built on a bend of the Euphrates River in Syria - some interesting evidence was revealed regarding Christian art. The ruins of a third century synagogue and Christian church were discovered there. Paintings found in both of these buildings provide us with information of the style and subjects that were being painted. In respect of these paintings at Dura-Europos as well as those that had been found in

the catacombs, it is interesting to note that there is a similarity in style as well as in the subjects depicted. We see images of the Virgin and of Christ. Although the Virgin appears in the form of a person, Christ is still represented by a symbol. A noticeable point about the form of the paintings at this stage though, is that they display a number of characteristics that we later find in the icon. Already the image is reduced to a minimum of detail. The subjects are not in profile but face to the front and there is no depth or shadow in the work. The faces are beginning to take on a look of spirituality.
Another form of painting which displays almost identical characteristics with the Dura-Europos and catacomb paintings and, which date from the same period, are the mummy portraits of Fayoum in Egypt. The illustration of the portrait of the young man from Fayoum shows a remarkable resemblance to the style of the icon and many historians consider these portraits to be the forerunners of the Christian icon. *(Plate 1)*

In the form and style of the paintings of Dura-Europos, the catacombs and the mummy portraits of Fayoum we are, therefore, by the third century already witnessing the emergence of the classical style of the Orthodox icon as we know it.

The Era of Constantine I

In 312 AD an event took place which totally transformed the outward situation of the church. The emperor, Constantine, was passing through Gaul with his army *en route* to what was to be the battle of Milvian Bridge. Constantine looked up into the sky and saw a flaming cross with the accompanying words, "In this sign, conquer". During the night Christ appeared to him holding in his hand the same image that the emperor had seen in the sky. Christ ordered him to place this image on his standard which was to lead the army into battle. Constantine was victorious and as a result of this vision he became the first Roman emperor to embrace Christianity. His conversion brought to an end the persecution of Christians and so, this primitive religion which had formally been conducted in such secrecy was now to become the religion of the new Christian empire in the East. This occurred in 324 AD when Constantine took the decision to move the capital of the Roman empire from Italy to the site of the Greek city of Byzantium on the shores of the Bosphorus in present-day Turkey. He changed the name of the city to Constantinople in honour of himself. In 325 he presided over an important church council at Nicaea as he had decided that if his new empire was to be a Christian one, he wanted it to be a Christian one firmly based upon one Orthodox faith. The council at Nicaea, therefore, had the role of deciding what the content of that faith would be. The first steps had now been taken which would lead to the establishment of the Christian empire of Byzantium.

The conversion of Constantine led to the emergence of a far greater following for Christianity. It also led to a transformation in sacred art. Throughout the empire many artists now worked exclusively for the glory of the new faith. A new style of art emerged that was essentially Christian although its roots were Hellenistic and oriental. It received the name "Byzantine" and, during the next two centuries it was to find its definitive form.

It must be noted that up to this point the word "icon" had not yet been used to describe the holy images that were being painted. Although sacred art was taking on a host of new themes and forms and, had also found for itself a place in the life of the church, "Byzantine" art at this point did not in essence differ much from the art of the western part of the empire.

This was to change with the calling together of the Quinisext Council.

The Quinisext Council

In 692 the emperor Justinian II called together a council in Constantinople which was to have important implications for iconography. The council was called "Quinisext" because it completed the two ecumenical councils that preceded it; the fifth in 554 and the sixth in 681, both of which were held in Constantinople. The Quinisext was held in a "chamber" (in Trullo) of the imperial palace and for this reason it is often referred to as the "Council in Trullo". It was convened to discuss, amongst other matters, the question of heresies and false teachings within the church. Approximately 102 canons (decrees) concerning every aspect of church life were discussed. Three of these dealt directly with the question of sacred images. In earlier times Christ had on numerous occasions been portrayed as the "Good Shepherd". In the West, in particular, He had also been represented as a lamb. As mentioned earlier this imagery was often to be found in the catacombs. The council stated, ".... in order to expose to the sight of all, at least with the help of painting, that which is perfect, we decree that henceforth Christ our God be represented in His human form and not in the ancient form of the lamb". Canon 82 of the Quinisext Council, therefore, gives for the first time very clear direction to the church's teaching on the sacred image. The sacred image had now become an object of veneration for the entire church and was given equal status with the Holy Scriptures and the Cross.
It is from this moment that it becomes appropriate to use the word "icon" to describe these sacred images.

The Iconoclast Controversy

Soon after the conclusion of the Quinisext Council which allowed for the veneration of icons, a dispute broke out between the supporters of icons and those who were opposed to them. Those in favour of the icons - the iconodules - defended the place of icons in worship, whilst those opposed to them - the iconoclasts - sought the destruction of these images. They were against any type of religious art which represented human beings or God. The iconoclasts introduced their arguments by disputing an earlier standpoint of the Council of Chalcedon of 451 AD which had proclaimed that while Christ is a single, undivided person, He is not only from two natures but in two natures. The council had declared that the two natures of Christ were unconfused, unchanged, indivisible and inseparable and that there was no difference between the two natures because of this union. The individual property of each nature is preserved and both natures combine in one person - the *"hypostasis"* (person). The iconoclasts denied that the mystery of Christ included both his Divine and Human natures; in other words they rejected the concept of the *"hypostatic"* union. They asserted categorically that His humanity was absorbed by and, was subordinate to his Divinity. As an extension of this argument they stated that as no one had ever seen God, His image could not be depicted. So it can be seen that besides the standpoint that existed amongst the iconoclasts as to what could or could not be depicted in sacred art, there was also the issue of the character of Christ's human nature and, as a consequence, a view that the veneration of images *could,* in fact, constitute a degree of idolatry.

These views were unacceptable to those who defended the icons. They stated that the concept of the two natures of Christ could not be ignored and quite simply *must* be recognised. They argued that in an icon of Christ it was not just either His Divinity or His humanity which was represented, but His *complete* Person, uniting both natures "inseparably and without confusion". The iconoclasts, they argued, by denying Christ's humanity, were denying the Incarnation. Now, if the Incarnation is the basis for the icon, the icon reciprocally serves to affirm the Incarnation; so to deny the one is to deny the other. To deny both is to deny Christianity. This view, of course, had serious implications for the icon and was at the centre of the iconoclastic controversy.

Ironically, it was Muslim and Jewish ideas that gave impetus to the iconoclast crisis. In the seventh century Muslim Arabs conquered Syria and Palestine and after further advances besieged Constantinople only to be driven back by Emperor Leo III. In the territories that they occupied they were reasonably tolerant towards Christian images. It was the Jews at this point, however, who again began to believe strongly in the prohibition of the image as prescribed in Old Testament law. They now began to destroy images in their synagogues. This was followed by the actions of Caliph Yezid who in 723 ordered the removal of all icons in Christian churches within the territories he ruled. Besides Islam and Judaism there was also opposition from within Christianity itself. Many Christians still believed that icons were idolatrous. It was for this reason that the iconoclasts were to find much support from within the church for their views.

Visible iconoclasm within the Orthodox world began in 726 at the initiative of the state. It was in this year that Leo III, influenced by various bishops, took a stance against the veneration of icons. The emperor attempted to persuade the patriarch, St Germanus, to support his position, but the patriarch refused to sign any decree until the matter had been discussed at an ecumenical council. As a result of this Germanus was deposed and replaced by a supporter of iconoclasm - Patriarch Anastasius. The iconoclastic decree which was subsequently issued in 730 was signed by both the emperor and the patriarch. It, therefore, had state as well as church support. From this moment onwards icons began to be destroyed throughout the empire.

The first icon to be destroyed by order of the emperor was an icon of Christ above one of the entrances of the imperial palace. This act led to a popular uprising and a struggle began with much blood being spilt by both sides in the dispute. This iconoclastic struggle was to last for over one hundred years and can be divided into two periods. The first stretched from 730 to 787, whilst the second lasted from 814 to 843.

Church leaders responded swiftly to the iconoclastic decrees. Besides St Germanus' rejection of them, there were also reactions from Pope Gregory of Rome as well as from the patriarchs of Alexandria, Antioch and Jerusalem. The last mentioned patriarchs, however, could not do very much at the time as they were in territories occupied by Muslims. It was St John of Damascus though, who took up the defence of icons with the first of his three treatises on the subject.

The first period of iconoclasm reached its height during the reign of Constantine Copronymous, the son of Leo III. He was more fanatical than his father and during his reign many monks were cruelly persecuted. This resulted in many of them emigrating to places such as Cyprus and Italy. These persecutions subsided at his death and when his son and successor, Leo IV, died in 780 Leo's wife Irene came to the throne. She was an Orthodox who had never ceased venerating icons and so immediately set about restoring Orthodoxy. The Seventh Ecumenical Council convened in 787, at the end of the first period of the iconoclastic controversy, delivered the most complete teaching yet given on the icon. It was at this

council that the veneration of icons was re-established and the foundations for the theology of the icon were laid.
The debate on the theology of the icon is vast both in content and complexity and stands outside the scope of such a limited study as this. Nevertheless, in the deliberations of the council two overriding and recurring themes are given prominence - the element of the *Incarnation,* and the theology of "*presence*". In their discussions at the council, the Church Fathers made extensive use of the writings of St John of Damascus. He had been a great defender of icons and had set out his arguments in three treatises called *Apologetic Discourses to Those who Defame the Holy Icons.* They rank amongst the most in-depth expositions of the Orthodox view on the theology of the icon. In his discourses St John argued that by the Incarnation, the Old Testament prohibition of graven images had been abolished. He stated that in earlier times God, who is without body, could not have been depicted, but now through the Incarnation He had been seen in the flesh and it was because of this that an image of Him could be made. The distinction, of course, also had to be made between the veneration and the idolisation of this image.

Briefly put, it could be argued that the icon is not an object to be *worshipped* because it is not an idol. An icon differs from an idol because the latter is an image of a non-existent thing and bears no likeness to any original object or being. The icon is the opposite of this. It is a symbol, and the veneration shown towards it is *not* towards the paint or the panel, but towards the person represented. So when veneration is offered to the image of Christ, that veneration becomes worship not of the image, but of Christ. As the image of Christ, therefore, the icon shares in the mystery of both His humanity and His Divinity. The icon, therefore, is Christ's presence in our midst.

These teachings on the icon were not, however, accepted by everyone and it did not take long - twenty years, in fact, - for another period of violence against icons to break out. This was instigated by Leo V. Once again monks were persecuted whilst icons and sacred books were destroyed. In 842 Theodora became regent for Michael III who was the son of the iconoclastic emperor, Theophilus. Theodora was an Orthodox who had continued the veneration of icons during the intervening years. The veneration of icons was then re-established by a council held in Constantinople in 843 under Patriarch St Methodius. This council confirmed the dogma of the veneration of icons which had been brought about by the Seventh Ecumenical Council. The council excommunicated the iconoclasts and proclaimed in March 843 the feast of the Triumph of Orthodoxy. This feast is always celebrated on the first Sunday in Lent. The proclamation of the Triumph of Orthodoxy brought to an end the period of iconoclasm which had lasted some 120 years.

Beyond The Triumph of Orthodoxy

When icon painting resumed in the 9th century it was centred on what is now Turkey and Greece. Later, with the conversion to Orthodoxy of the Balkans these regions also became centres of icon painting. Towards the end of the 10th century, the conversion to Christianity of the Principality of Kiev began the spread of Orthodoxy and icon painting in Russia. Icon painting was also to flourish in Cyprus.

What follows here is a very brief outline of iconographic development in those lands which were influenced by Orthodoxy.

It will be appropriate to begin with Constantinople as it was here that most of the history of the icon up to this point had been focused. It is sad to say, however, that few icons from Constantinople remain. This is mainly due to iconoclasm; but in later years Venetian looting as well as the sack of the city by the Turks in 1453 contributed to this. Byzantine icon painting did, however, continue in Constantinople during the 13th century despite the founding of a Latin kingdom there. In the Palaeologan period (1261-1453) which began with the reconquest of Constantinople, icon painting was resumed on a large scale. During this period a very conscious return was made to the style of icon painting which had existed in the past. By the 14th and 15th centuries icon painting in Constantinople had reached a high level of artistry and it is the style of icons from this period that is most imitated.

During the Byzantine era Thessaloniki in Greece was an important city. Although it came under the cultural influence of Constantinople it did develop some characteristics of its own. Greece, however, had to succumb on occasions to invaders whose own religion was in conflict with Orthodoxy and this resulted in icon painting taking place in far-flung centres rather than the traditional ones. It was in remote places such as Meteora and on Mount Athos - the Holy Mountain - that icon painting flourished. After a period of prolonged decline and a relative lack of large scale activity, Greek iconography was to come into its own again during the iconographic renewal of the twentieth century.

Icon painting in Macedonia and Serbia was influenced by the work being done in Constantinople. The earliest icons in Macedonia are to be found in the city of Ohrid. These date from 1037 when many artists came to the city to work on the restoration of the archiepiscopal church of St Sophia. The Serbs, on the other hand, although being influenced by Constantinople, were keen to produce their own distinctive style of iconography. They attempted to do this

by promoting the cult of local bishops. Although they imitated the style of Byzantine iconographers they introduced style and features depending on the environment in which they were working.
It is not known with a great deal of certainty when icon painting started in Cyprus, but records suggests that icons were kept in churches as early as the 8th century. During its history Cyprus fell under various influences and these are reflected in the styles of icon painting. Icon painting there reached its climax in the 12th century. By then the island had become an important military centre of Byzantium and many of the military personnel who governed the island associated their names with monasteries and churches. This gave an impetus to icon painting which flourished as never before. With the fall of Constantinople in 1453 many icon painters sought refuge in Cyprus where they were welcomed and supported by Queen Helena Palaeologina, a niece of the last Byzantine emperor. The 12th and 13th centuries were thus marked by the pure Byzantine style under the influence of these refugees. With the institution of Venetian rule on the island from 1487 to 1570 icon painting was influenced by contemporary Italian painting. This amalgamation of traditional Byzantine painting with Gothic and Renaissance art created a pure Cypriot style in the late 15th and 16th centuries.

In 988 the conversion to Christianity of the Principality of Kiev began the spread of icon painting in what is present-day Russia. The first icons in Kiev were of the Constantinople style. When the Mongols conquered the principality during the 13th century, artistic development there came to an end. Russian links with Byzantium were not, however, entirely severed as iconic traditions continued and developed in Novgorod to the north, as well as in Pskov.
By the 14th century Moscow had become the centre of artistic production. A number of Greek artists had come to work in the city,

one of whom was Theophanes. He had also worked in Novgorod so his style was a blend of the Novgorod and the Constantinople schools. By the mid-15th century Moscow had become the capital of Russia and when Constantinople fell in 1453, she considered herself to be the "Third Rome" and the "Guardian" of Byzantium. The icons painted during the 14th and 15th centuries in Moscow are considered to be the high point of icon painting in Russia. It was during the 15th century that Andrei Rublev appeared on the scene. His work is regarded as exhibiting an extension and refinement of the style of Constantinople. He is popularly regarded as the greatest iconographer and his most famous work, The Holy Trinity, can be seen by visitors to Russia. Although moves have been made to return it to a church or monastery it *may* still be in the Tretiakov Gallery in Moscow where it was originally displayed. Icon painting connected with him dominated the first part of the 15th century and in the latter part of the century it became virtually the only artistic current. The church, in fact, officially instructed painters to follow his style.

In the 16th century in Russia icons began to be produced in greater quantities than ever before. The style had become more delicate and fragile. The leading figure in this style was Dionysii. It is during this period that icon workshops were established and icon-painting schools were founded by wealthy merchants such as the Strogonov family. Icons of quality continued to be painted in Russia up to the end of the 16th century. The so-called "guardian" of Russian icon painting was considered to be one Father Makary who later became the Metropolitan of Moscow and All Russia. He had trained as an icon painter and assisted in the establishment of many icon-painting schools.

After the fall of Constantinople in 1453 the subjugated Greeks were divided between the Ottoman Empire and the Republic of Venice.

Many icon painters now took refuge on Crete which was under Venetian domination. Here they were allowed to continue with their icon painting which later developed into a "post-Byzantine" school producing outstanding works through people such as Andreas and Nicholas Ritzos, Nicholas Tzafuris and Emmanuel Tzanes. It was, however, during the successive decades that contact with the West through the Venetian influence resulted in dilution of the typical Byzantine style; and ultimately we can start to talk of a Greco-Italian style rather than a Cretan style.

By 1500 the western influences through the impact of the Italian Renaissance had become more noticeable and were to be found particularly in icons being painted in Venice as well as in the icons of an Italo-Byzantine school in Cyprus. During this time Serbia and Russia as well as Mount Athos continued to develop distinctive features in their icon painting whilst respecting the fundamental ideas and iconography derived from Constantinople. After the Turkish conquest of the Balkans and the fall of Serbia in 1459, icon painting in these regions went into decline. This happened because many of the wealthy patrons who had formally commissioned icons moved on as did many of the iconographers who had painted them. The main icon centres were now in Russia, Venice and Crete. In the 16th century icons were being painted in all Orthodox lands, but by now the western influence was becoming fairly dominant.

The quality and style of icon painting began to go into an accelerated decline during the 17th century. This was again largely due to the western influence that brought about the abandonment of the tradition which dictated how icons should be painted. It was asserted that this "abandonment of tradition" caused a diminution in the levels of spirituality which were an essential element in the paintings. Although the Eastern Church attempted to remain faithful to the two-dimensional aspect of iconography which is regarded as

being more accessible to mystery, the Western Church shifted towards three-dimensionality. Attempts were now being made to present landscapes and a more realistic relationship between man and nature. In addition, the use of perspective undermined the fundamental aspect of the icon.
The decline was now almost complete and icon painting was to lie largely dormant until the iconographic renewal in the twentieth century which was set in motion by monks Gregory Kroug and Leonid Ouspensky as well as Photius Kontoglou who is credited with having initiated the revival of the Byzantine tradition in Greece.

This last section has been but the briefest of surveys of iconographic activities in those lands which fell under Orthodox influence. The intention in each case has been to highlight one or two significant developments. Mention has barely even been made of the iconic tradition in Bulgaria, Georgia, Moldavia and Romania. Then there are the icons of the Crusader period, whilst Coptic icons also deserve a study in their own right. For a more detailed study of the various traditions, it is strongly suggested that further reference is made to the specialist literature available.

2

THE FEATURES OF ICONS

Many people newly introduced to icons may wonder why in iconography there appears to be a particular, limited range of subjects depicted and that wherever they may see them, these icons seem to be almost identical in style and execution. The answer to this is quite simple. Strict guidelines have been laid down for the iconographer to follow and from which he should not digress. Leonid Ouspensky emphasises this point when he says,
"....*Reverently preserving the memory of the Saints and their characteristics, the Orthodox Church has never accepted the painting of their icons from the imagination of the artist or from a living model, for this would involve a complete and conscious rupture with the prototype, and the prototype with whose name the icon is inscribed would be arbitrarily replaced by another person".*[1]

The Prototype

When we talk of the prototype being referred to, above, we are talking of the *original* icon of a particular subject painted by the *ancient* iconographers. In other words it is essential that every newly-painted icon of a holy figure resembles as closely as possible every *previous* image of that figure. It can be seen, therefore, that the subject of an icon is never simply "invented" by an iconographer in some random manner according to his own imagination.

---

[1] Ouspensky L. Lossky V: *The Meaning of Icons;* Page 37

Many of the prototypes were established by iconographers who had personal experience of the subjects they were painting. They were familiar with the appearance of these subjects as very often they had actually been present at the particular event they were painting. A majority of the icons depicting these great events or festivals, for example, date from the early centuries of Christianity and were originally painted in the localities where they took place. It is for this reason that the church regards these subjects and the way they are depicted as historically correct. These are the iconic subjects, therefore, that became prototypes and are works upon which subsequent icons were based.

In 787 a decree of the Seventh Ecumenical Council stated that only the technical aspect of the icon depended on the painter; its design, disposition and composition depended quite clearly on the Holy Fathers. By the Holy Fathers we mean those churchmen and theologians for whom the Orthodox church has special reverence and who have played a particularly significant role in helping to formulate the canons and Traditions of the church. The Orthodox church has never attempted to define exactly who these Holy Fathers are, but clearly they would include such eminent theologians as John of Damascus, for example, who - as we will recall - was one of the chief defenders of icons during the iconoclastic period. By establishing these canons and directing iconographers to conform to them, the Holy Fathers of the Orthodox church were laying down guidelines and safeguards that were designed to guarantee spiritual continuity and doctrinal unity. The ancient, as well as those future iconographers were, after all, depicting Christ and the Saints in their work and, quite naturally, it was crucial to the Church that the subjects never became caricatures. The sacred canons, therefore, established and defined the themes of icons according to Tradition and ensured that the subjects were not the outcome of the iconographer's own creativity and imagination. Much later, in 1551, this idea was taken a step further when the Muscovite "Council of One Hundred Chapters" declared, "....Archbishops and bishops in all cities, villages and monasteries of their dioceses will supervise icon painters and personally examine their works". By doing this attempts were made to establish existing works, or new prototypes of well-known iconographers, as patterns for future iconographers.

Painters' Manuals

In order not to digress from Tradition, thereby remaining true to the established canons, various manuals began to appear over the succeeding centuries which were designed to give iconographers details and instructions on how to paint and produce the features of the subjects they were painting. These manuals, known as *Podlinniks* in Russia, gave precise details of features as well as basic colours to be used. The most famous manual of this type is regarded as that of the Athonite monk, Dionysius of Fourna, who was a monk on Mount Athos, the Holy Mountain. It was compiled in the 17th century at the request of the monks there. Interestingly, an iconographers "pattern book" in the Stroganov tradition also exists. This sourcebook of iconography dates from the 15th century. The Stroganovs were leaders of Moscow court life who were responsible for bringing some of the great Russian artists and scholars of the age together. Their role was to design iconic compositions representing biblical events which were then painted according to their specific guidelines in the icon workshops of the Stroganov family. The strict adherence to guidelines is crucial, therefore almost everything in the icon is depicted in the way that it is because it carries deep symbolic meaning. It should now be clearer that iconographic canon determines not only the subject of an icon, but also fixes how it should be depicted. This includes clothing styles, colours, gestures and numerous other details which will be covered as we proceed.

Technical Features

One of the first things a person will notice when examining an icon closely is the two-dimensional nature of the work as well as a certain absence of realism. By excluding attempts to create an illusion of real space and volume, the two-dimensional iconographic surface is believed to give a greater sense of mystery to the icon; and by disregarding all unnecessary detail in the subject being painted the iconographer is better able to capture the spiritual sense of the work where both time and space are lost and, therefore, have no meaning. Because of this convention we often see odd forms in iconography; and because depth does not really exist in an icon, everything, in essence, takes place in the "foreground". In many cases there will be no background scenery and the figure being depicted will simply be painted on a gold "background". Because time and space are excluded, the figures assume a greater degree of spirituality thereby immediately attracting our attention.

Iconic perspective is not bound by conventional rules and more often than not is simply ignored. When it *is* used we will often notice that a number of different types of perspective are used in the same icon. A common feature of this perspective is that it is often reversed. This means that the vanishing point is situated in front of the picture rather than behind. *(Diagram 1)* This reversed - or inverse perspective as it is also known - together with a number of other odd features is clearly visible in the icon of the Annunciation. *(Plate 2)* The bases of the columns and the canopy of the structure housing the Virgin's stool, for example, have different projections; whilst behind the angels we look down upon the roof of a building drawn

in inverse perspective. Also, what has happened to the right-hand column of the structure as we look at the composition ?
Architecture in icons also seems to ignore convention. No attention is given to correct proportions. Doors and windows often appear in wrong places and their size does not correspond to their function. Certain structures appear in the composition that do not seem to have any particular purpose. Scenes which take place within a building are always shown with the building as the background. A red curtain draped between buildings indicates that the scene is taking place inside. The icon does not use shadows in its art. Those parts of the building that are in shadow are not painted as such but are painted in flat colour. Mountains and vegetation in icons, like the architecture, are represented as background props and are always of less importance than the people depicted in the foreground. The illustration of the icon representing Christ's entry into Jerusalem gives a good idea of how buildings, mountains, vegetation and animals are represented in icons. *(Plate 3)* The positioning of a person is also sometimes of significance and very often a person standing in the "background" can be larger than a person standing in the "foreground".

Sacred Geometry

A knowledge of geometry is required by any iconographer as there is a well-defined structure underlying the composition of all icons. This refers, in particular, to the proportions of the body and the face. Even a composition with a number of figures will comply with geometric forms such as the triangle, circle, square or rectangle. *(Diagram 2)* This all contributes to the divine harmony of the composition. Our knowledge of this geometry is to be found in ancient manuals and although various geometric proportions have changed during the centuries, the "sacred geometry" underlying the composition has played a vital role in conveying the spiritual meaning of the icon.

Colours

Colours play a very important part in iconography and are used according to the symbolic significance that they have. The iconographer cannot use colours according to his whims, but is dictated to by the established canons. This explains why icons of the same subject but from different eras and schools are always painted in the same colours. These colours are always bright and very often the unusual choice of colour for certain subjects is designed to emphasise a lack of realism thereby giving the composition a more spiritual and mystical nature. Although the subject of colour merits a study in its own right, it will be appropriate at this point to make mention of just one colour - *gold* - which is arguably the most significant of all the colours used. Its use is inextricably linked to the concept of "light" which is *the* overriding theme of icons. It is the "background" of an icon which is, *in fact,* called its "light" and, it is gold that is used to convey this concept. It is not a colour seen in everyday nature so for this reason the golden background of the icon gives the impression of creating an environment where bodies no longer need to conform to earthly rules. Freed from these earthly properties they assume a certain feeling of spirituality. Also, we must remember that gold is unlike other colours, which are *refractions* of pure light. Gold is light *itself* and for this reason it symbolises Divinity. Particularly in the domes of Byzantine churches we note the liberal use of gold. Here, the gold - as in icons - symbolises the world beyond; a world where "the sun never sets". In icons gold is always used in places where Holiness or Divinity is emphasised and, it should now be better appreciated why it is used to such an extent in the "background" of icons. Quite simply, gold is *not* like other colours. It does not *come* from light. It *is* light and, as stated earlier, light is *the* theme of icons.

The Figures in the Composition

This brings us to the figures in the composition. The size of a figure is usually determined by its importance. The bodies are often quite elongated and always face the front. Only people who have not attained holiness are seen in profile. By their frontality the figures in the icon are able to receive the word of God face to face. The foreheads are often quite high in order to convey the power of the Spirit and of Wisdom. The eyes are large and give the impression of staring. This is designed to fascinate the person looking at the icon. The ears are always shown uncovered as they are created to listen to and hear the commandments of the Lord. The nose is thin and elongated which gives a certain nobility to the face. The lips are always drawn finely and geometrically in order to eliminate any sensuality. The mouth is always closed as true contemplation demands silence. The throat and neck are always visible and are disproportionately large. A line indicates the Adams apple.

The hands are always held in a symbolic way; they are either blessing, praying or pointing to God. The fingers are not naturalistic; they are always long and pointed. Like the elongated nature of the bodies, this is designed to indicate a certain degree of de-materialisation. It contributes towards the spirituality of the figure. Similarly, if it should happen that the figure be depicted in the nude - as in the icon of the Baptism of Christ - the lack of naturalism in the figure is aimed at rendering it more spiritual in appearance.

The folds in the clothing of the figures may often look abstract and arbitrary; but they are, in fact, meant to express the physical as well as the spiritual movement of the figure. The folds make complete logical sense and where the garment or robe touches the Holy body, it radiates energy and light. The figure is completed by having a gold halo around the head which symbolises its Divinity.

In certain icons such as the Resurrection, Ascension and Transfiguration, the figure of Christ is in the centre of circles of blue-white light. This is called a mandorla. It is usually circular in shape, but is sometimes represented as almond-shaped and, on occasions, colours other than blue-white are used. *(Plate 4)* Not all icons of Christ necessarily have mandorlas; they usually appear only when a spectacular breakthrough of Divine Light is represented. A mandorla is similar in function to a halo and serves as the iconic representation of the uncreated light such as the disciples experienced during Christ's Transfiguration on Mount Tabor.

In a number of compositions it will be noticed that the persons depicted are standing - or are seated - with their feet on a rug, footrest or pedestal. This feature has a number of symbolic meanings. It usually indicates that the particular person has attained holiness. Also, however, it means to show in certain instances that the scene is taking place on *earth* rather than on a heavenly plane. Compositions with Christ seated on a throne always show Him with His feet placed on a footrest. This further emphasises His Lordship "....The heaven *is* my throne, and the earth *is* my footstool...."
(Is. 66:1)

By now it will be clear that the strict canons laid down for the iconographer to follow are not there to restrict him in any way, but are meant to free him to concentrate on the essential requirements which are designed to enable the icon to convey the highest degree of spirituality.

Despite fidelity to iconographic tradition, icons are still, however, never quite identical as a certain degree of latitude is permissible in producing a defined iconographic subject.

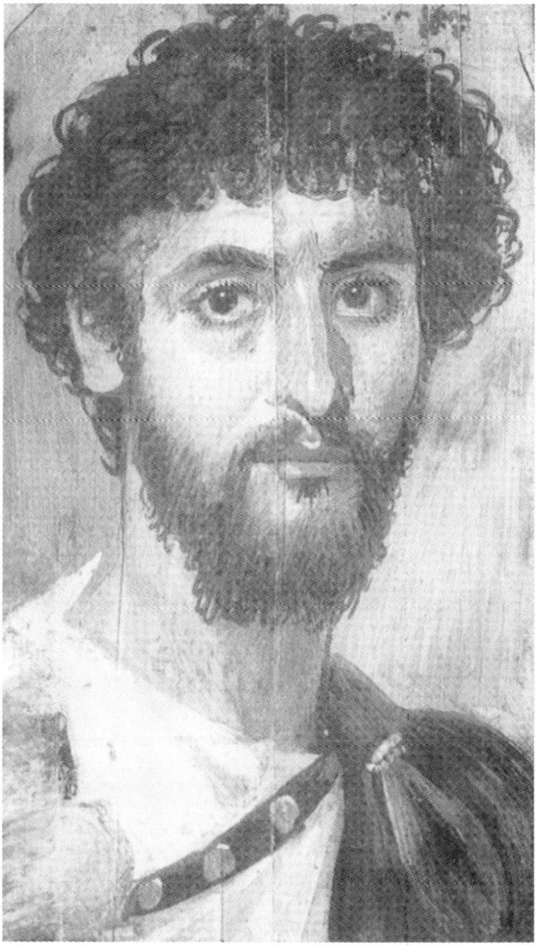

Plate 1. Fayoum Portrait

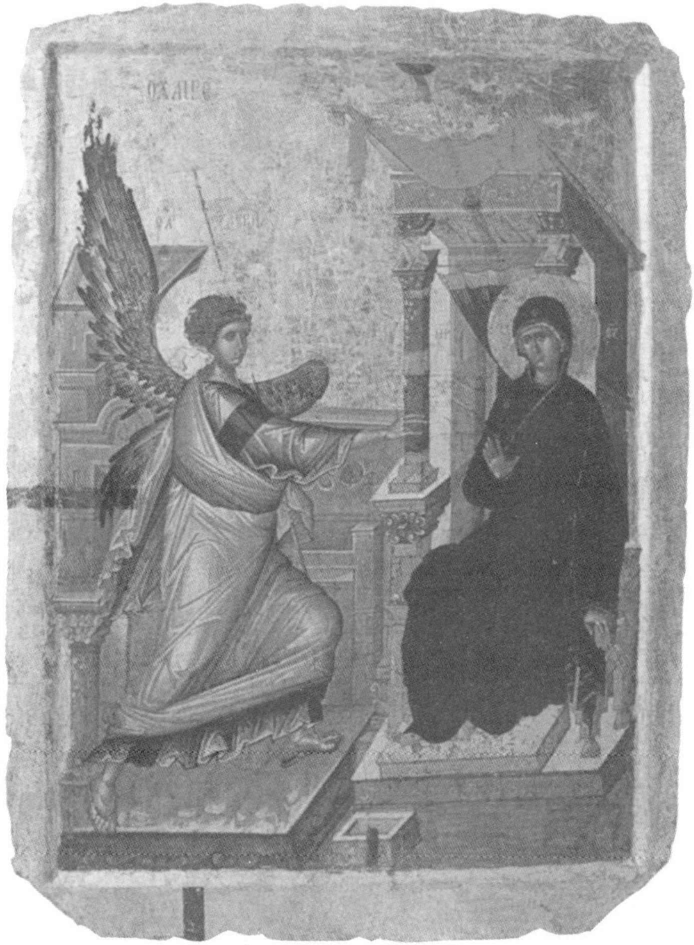

Plate 2. The Annunciation

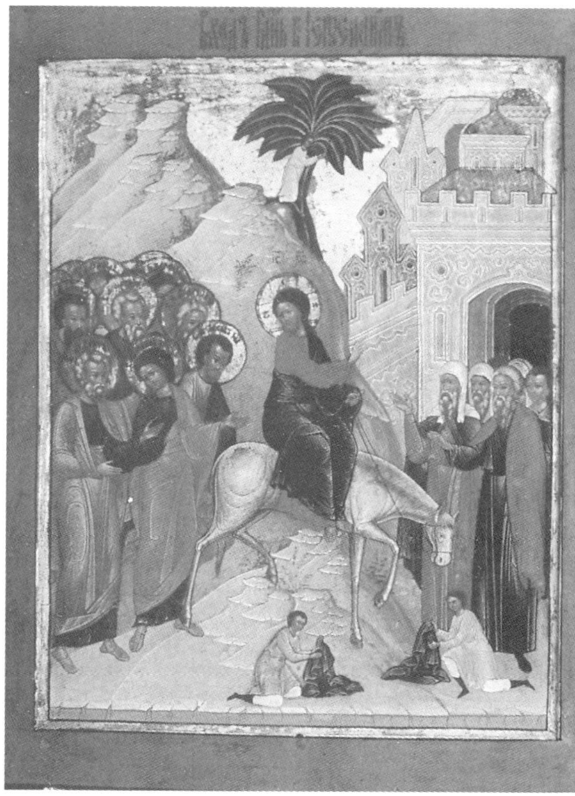

Plate 3. Christ's entry into Jerusalem

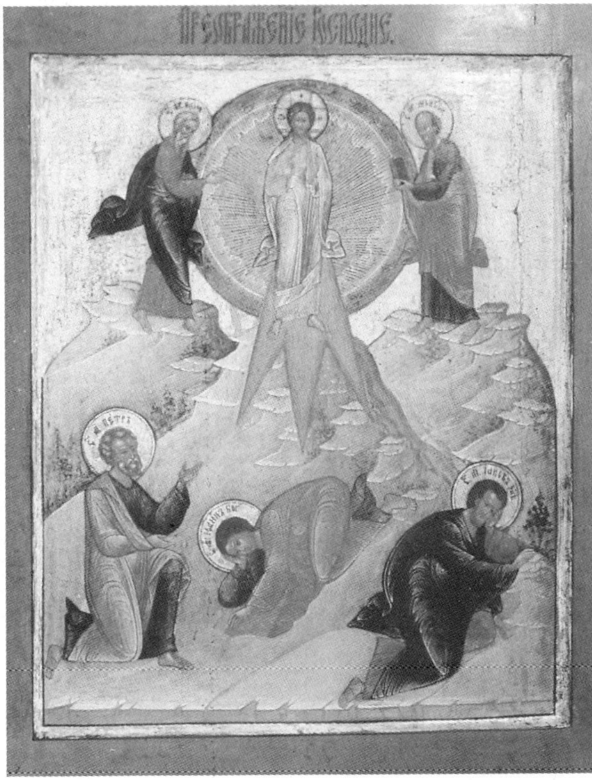

Plate 4. The Transfiguration

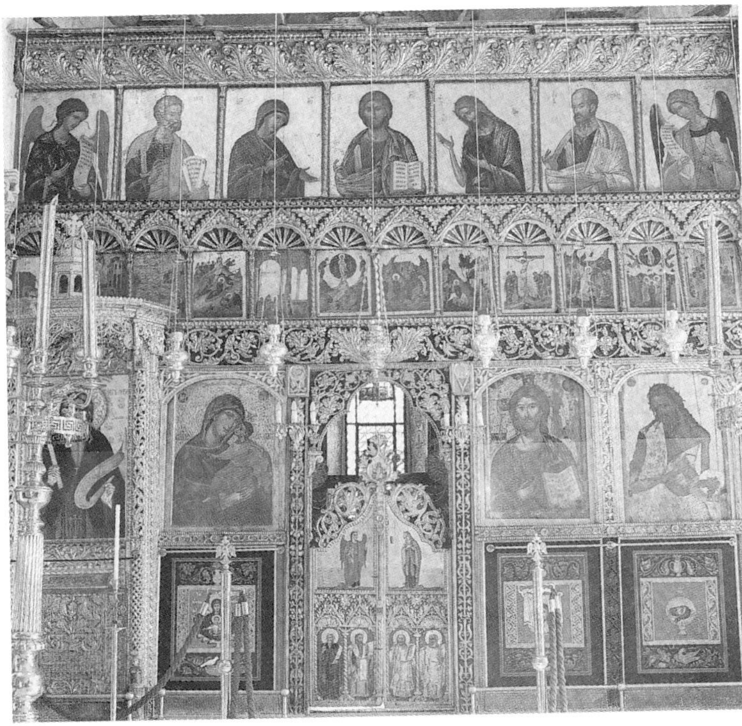

Plate 5. An Iconostasis

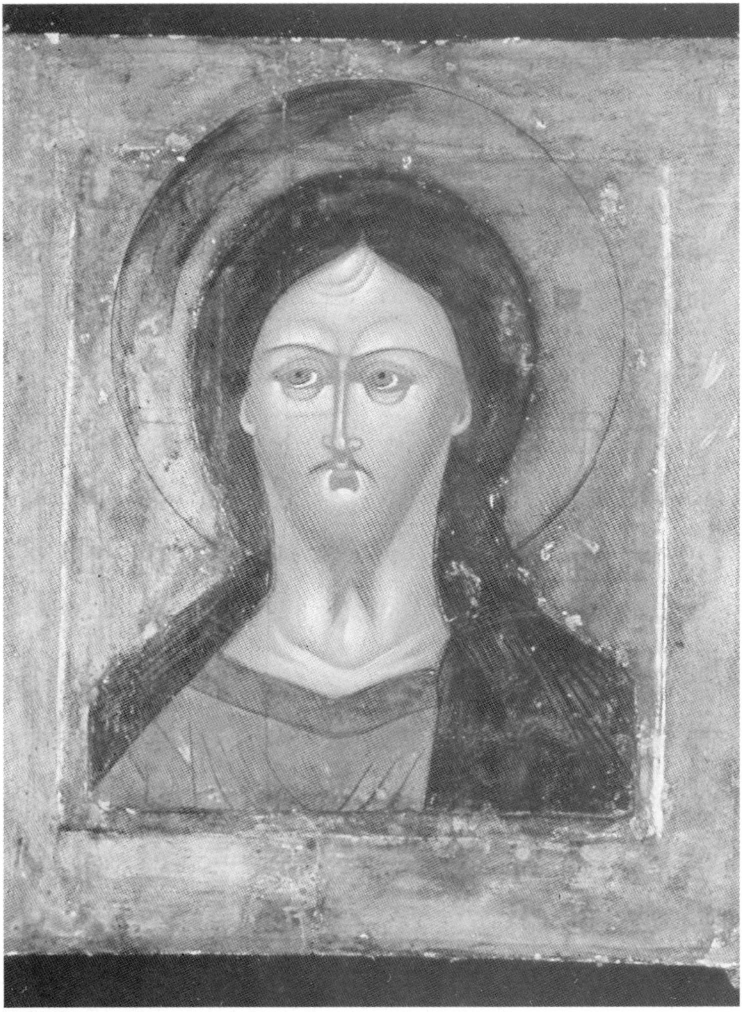

Plate 6. Christ

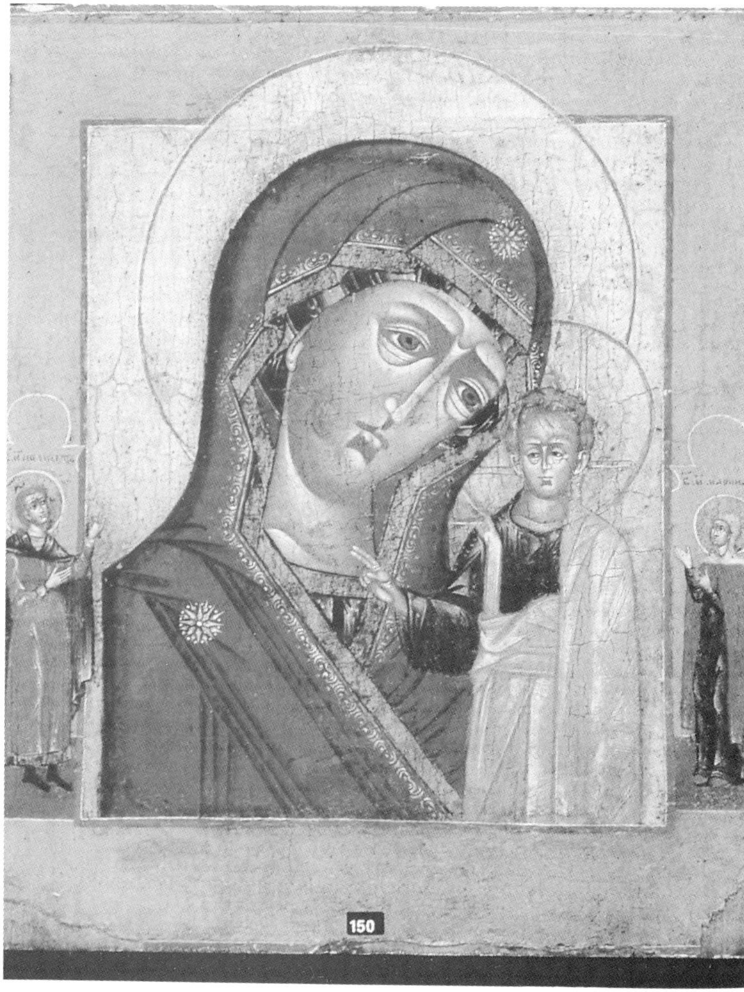

Plate 7. Mother of God

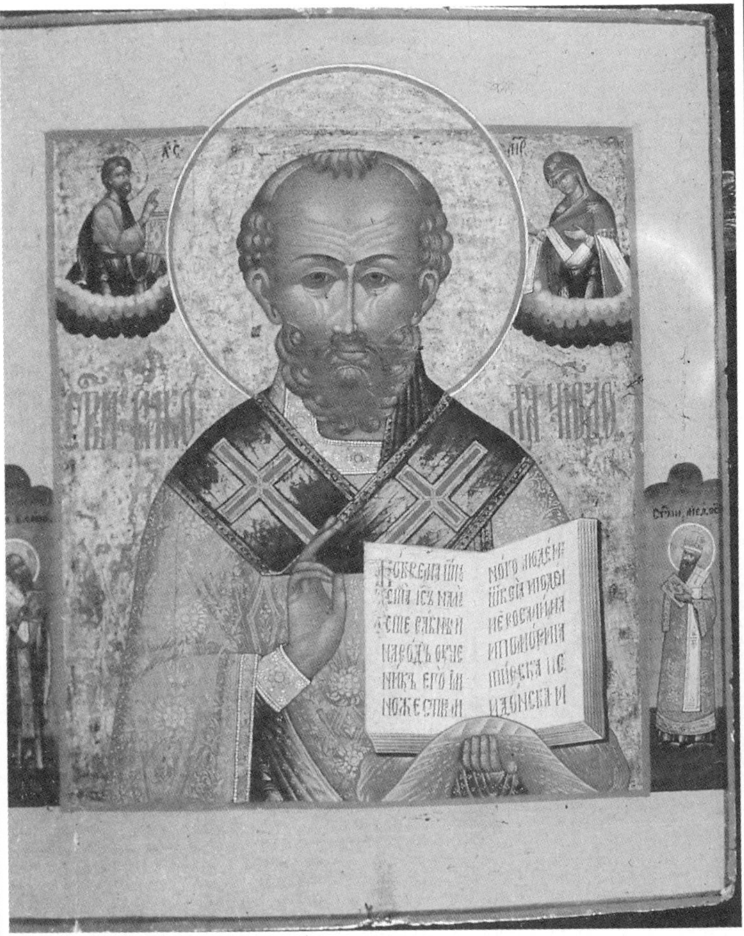

Plate 8. St Nicholas

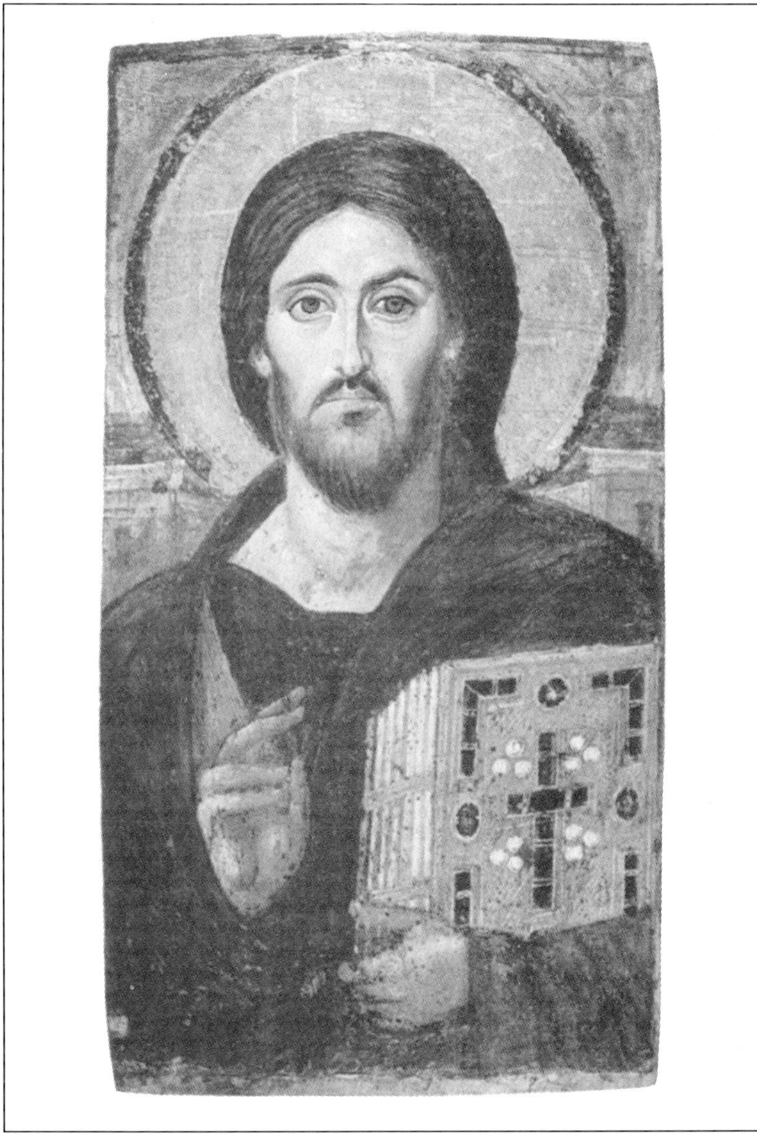

Plate 9. The"Sinai" Christ

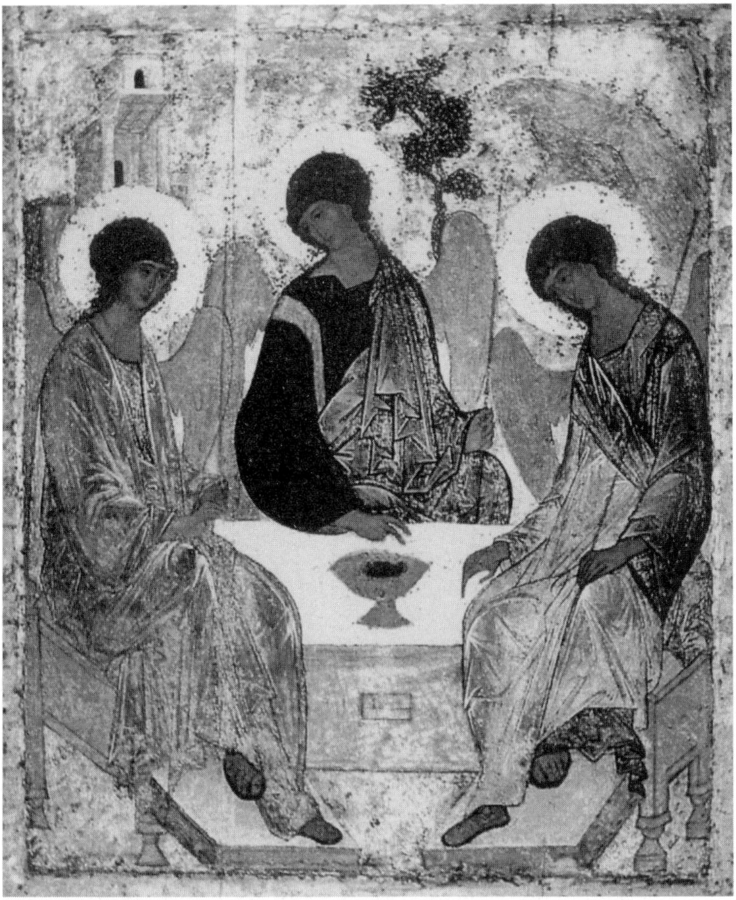

Plate 10. Rublev's Holy Trinity

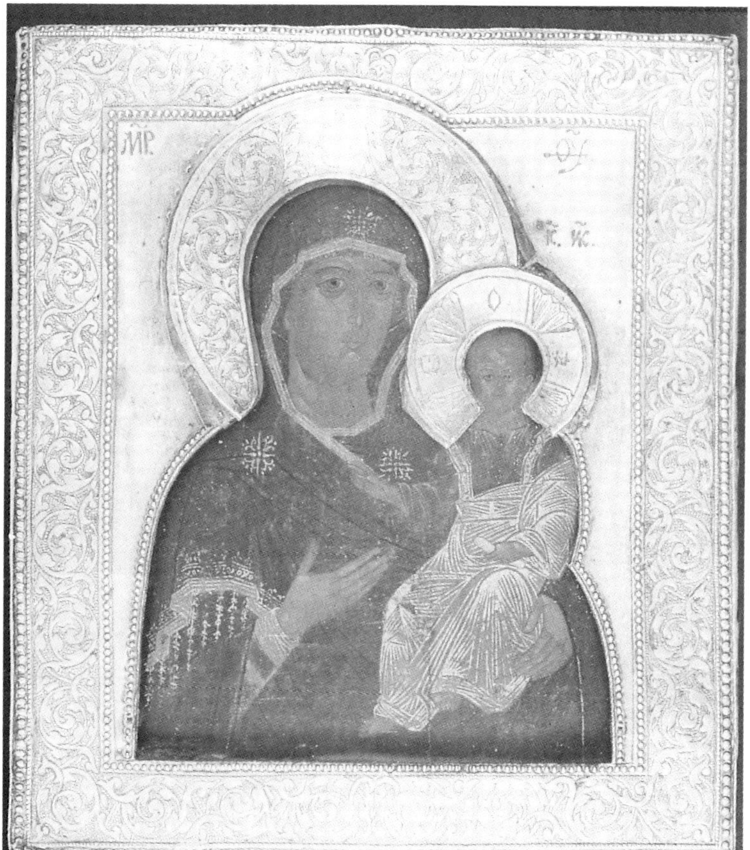

Plate 11. An "Oklad" covered icon of the Mother of God

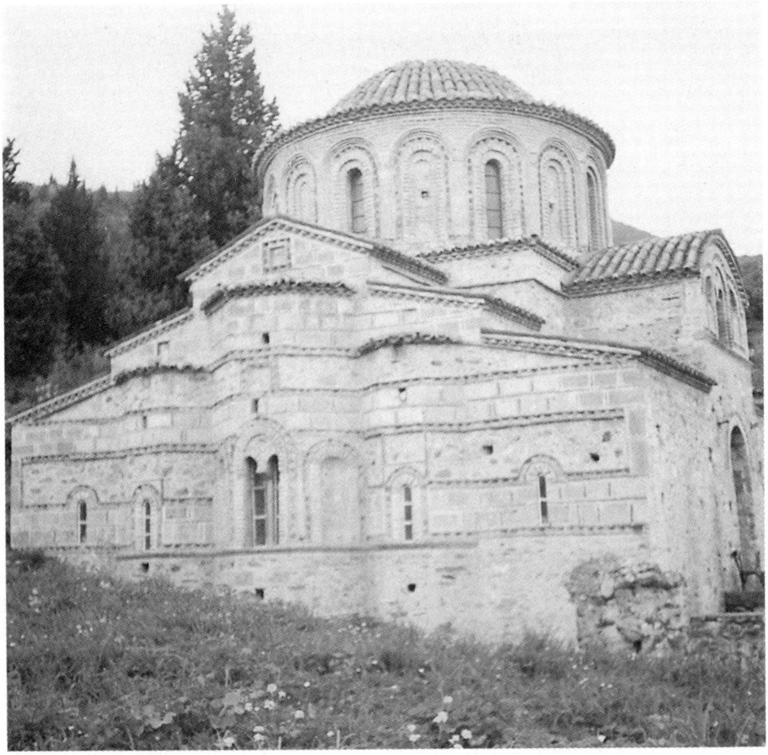

Plate12. Byzantine-style Church architecture

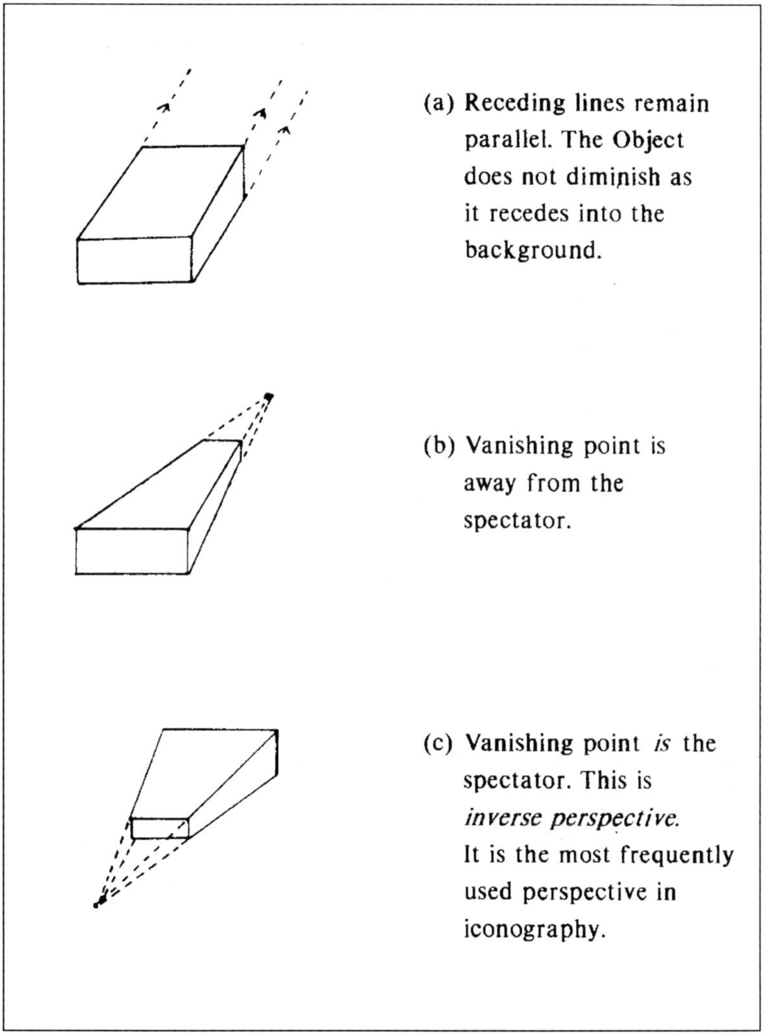

Diagram 1. Types of perspective

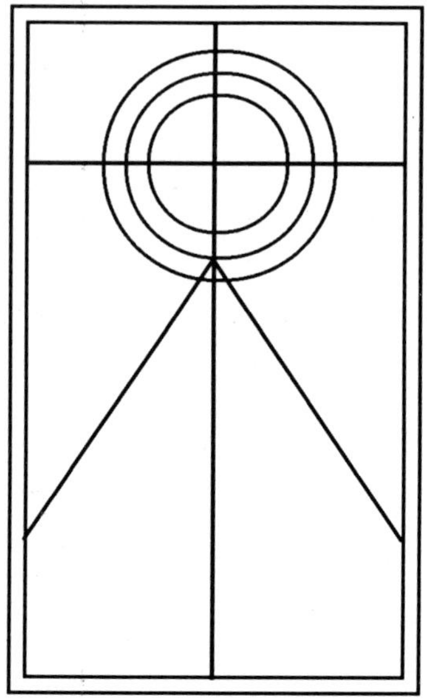

Diagram 2. The sacred geometry underlying the icon of the Transfiguration (see Plate 4).

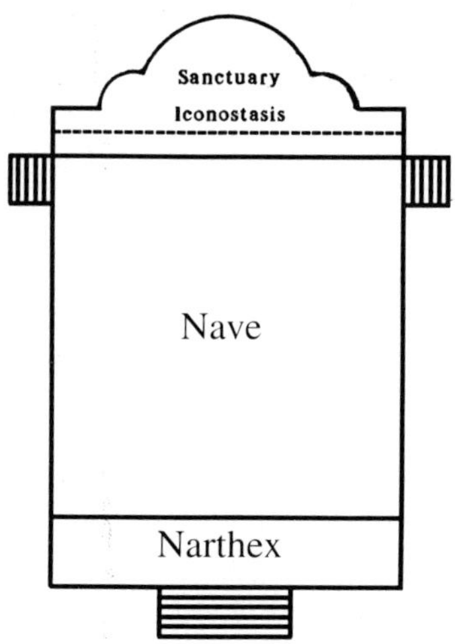

Diagram 3. The ground plan of a typical Orthodox Church

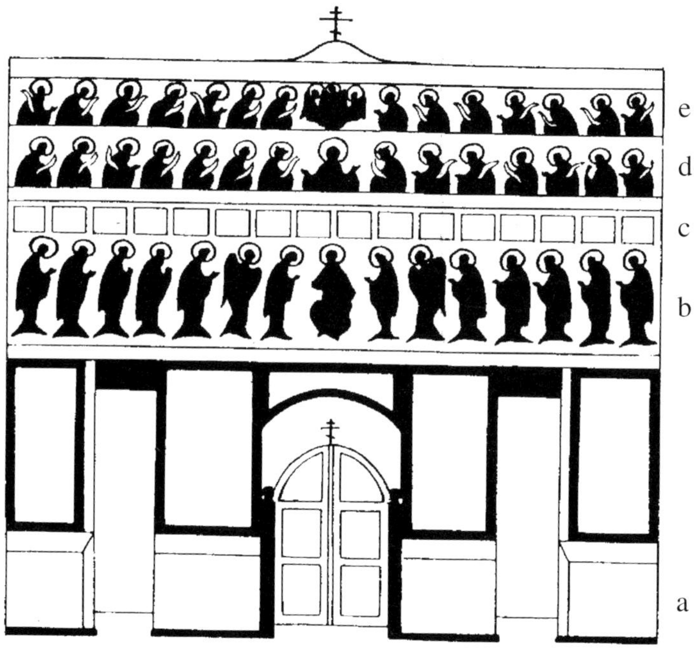

(a) Lowest level with Royal or Holy Door

(b) “Tchin”

(c) The Liturgical Feasts

(d) The Prophets

(e) The Patriarchs

Diagram 4. A Classic Iconostasis

Other Saints	St Peter	Archangel Gabriel	The Mother of God	Christ	St John the Baptist	Archangel Michael	St Paul	Other Saints

Diagram 5. The Order of Succession on the "Tchin"

IC XC - Jesus Christ

ΜΡ ΘΥ - Mother of God.

Ο ΑΡΧ - The Archangel.

Ο ΑΓ - The Saint

Η ΟΔΗΓΗΤΡΙΑ - Hodigitria.

Ο ΠΑΝΤΟΚΡΑΤΩΡ - Pantocrator.

Ο Ω Ν - "The Being". This inscription appears inside the halo of Christ.

Diagram 6. Some familiar inscriptions appearing in icons

3

THE ICON IN WORSHIP

Religious Symbolism of Church Architecture

One of the most distinctive aspects of Orthodoxy is the prominent place which it has given to icons in the act of worship. Before having a look at how icons are incorporated in worship it will be useful to look at the symbolism of the church building in which they are found.

An Orthodox church is usually rectangular in plan. It is divided into three parts - the sanctuary, the nave and the narthex - according to the plan of the tabernacle of Moses and the temple of Solomon. The sanctuary is the most important part of the church and is reserved for the clergy. It is where the Eucharist takes place. Symbolically the sanctuary represents the "House of God". It corresponds to the "Holy of Holies" in the tabernacle. The wide, central part of the church, the nave, corresponds to the "Holy" of the tabernacle which was separated from the courtyard by a veil. The nave is topped by a dome. The narthex corresponds to the courtyard of the tabernacle. *(Diagram 3)*

Another way of viewing this symbolism is to refer to the narthex as corresponding to the earth, the nave to heaven and the sanctuary to what is "above heaven". All the icons as well as biblical scenes executed in the form of frescoes, murals or mosaics that appear inside the church are arranged in accordance with this symbolism. Nothing is arranged at random. Each icon has its ordained place and is arranged according to a specific theme. The vertical dimensions of the building reflect the cosmic order and the paintings covering the walls - icons, frescoes or murals - tie in with this concept. The ground level represents the earth, whilst the upper parts of the walls and the ceiling represent the heavens. The Christ figure always adorns the large dome over the nave, whilst on the vaulting of the sanctuary the Mother of God is portrayed. This style of church architecture and decorative scheme has been adopted as the basis for the entire Orthodox world.

The Iconostasis

The most striking feature of any Orthodox church is the iconostasis, which is the screen composed of icons which separates the sanctuary from the nave. *(Plate 5)* All of the icons on the iconostasis are arranged in accordance with a particular symbolism and play a very important part in the liturgical rite of the church. Although the iconostasis is seen as dividing the Divine world from the human world it is at the same time also seen as uniting these two worlds. The symbolism of the icon on the iconostasis is to reveal to the worshipper how a reconciliation can be achieved between God and humankind.

It is sometimes suggested that the iconostasis cuts the worshippers off from the mystery of the Eucharist. Michel Quenot questions this view when he states, "*....By no means a barrier, the iconostasis is, positively speaking, the maximal expression of all that an icon can reveal to us visually. Behind it there is nothing to be seen. Why? Simply because the wondrous mystery that is celebrated there could never be situated on our own human, visual level so to speak; such a wondrous mystery is perceived not by human eyes, but by the soul in communion."*[2]

---

[2] Quenot, M: *The Icon: Windows on the Kingdom:* Page 48

The classic iconostasis which we find in churches today has up to five tiers or rows of icons. Typically, it consists of the following tiers: *(Diagram 4)*

The lowest level (a) has the Royal, or Holy Door in the centre. Only the priest and those assisting at the Eucharist are permitted to pass through these doors. Depicted on the doors are scenes of the Annunciation and the four Evangelists. The door symbolises the entry into the Kingdom of God, whilst the Annunciation marks the beginning of our salvation. The essential icons on the bottom tier are those immediately to the left and right of the doors. On the right of the door is the icon of Christ, or the icon of the event or person to whom the church is dedicated. On the left is the icon of the Mother of God. (As we look at the iconastasis)

The next tier (b) is called the "*Tchin*" - which means order. Its theme is of the Deësis - which means prayer - and consists of Christ enthroned in the centre with the Mother of God on the left and John the Baptist on the right standing in prayer before Christ. On either side of them arranged in strict order are a succession of Saints standing in prayer before Christ. *(Diagram 5)*

The next tier (c) shows the liturgical feasts. These icons represent the events of the New Testament.

Above this is the row of Prophets (d). In their hands they hold scrolls on which are written texts from their prophesies concerning the Incarnation.

The uppermost tier (e) consists of images of the Patriarchs. These are the forefathers representing the original church of the Old Testament.

Icons are also found elsewhere in the church; on the walls, in special shrines as well as on a stand at the entrance of the nave. This is where the icon of the patron saint of the church is placed. All of these icons play an integral part in the act of worship.

Orthodox worshippers on entering a church will go up to an icon, cross themselves, kiss the icon and light a candle in front of it. They may even prostrate themselves in front of one. During the service icons are frequently censed as well as carried in procession. The idea is to bring the faithful closer to the congregation of heaven. The worshippers, surrounded by the beautiful frescoes and icons, are meant to feel that they are in the presence of the heavenly congregation. The brilliance of the golden background of the icons which is enhanced by being surrounded by the glow of the candles and sanctuary lamps serves to radiate a light which is symbolic of the eternity of the world beyond this present one - the world to which the worshippers aspire.

Other incidences of the incorporation of icons in worship are to be seen in the use of the festal (festival) icons on days designated for their special use in celebrating the great feasts of the Orthodox Church. There are, in addition, miracle-working icons which play an important liturgical role. On days set aside for their special use they are usually carried in procession - often through the streets of the town or village of the church where they are kept. One such place is the Aegean island of Tinos which has become the spiritual centre of modern Greece. The focus of the worship on the island is an icon of the Virgin which is housed in the church of Panagia Evangelistra in the main town of the island. On the two great feasts of the Virgin - 25th March and the 15th August - many faithful who are in ill-health visit the church to be cured by the miracle-working icon.

Icons, therefore, are seen as the *total* expression of Orthodoxy. They are equivalent to the scriptural word and no part of the service can take place without their involvement as they complement the words spoken in the Divine Liturgy.

4

THE MAIN SUBJECTS OF ICONS

As we begin to know icons better we may ask ourselves where the iconographers gained the inspiration for their work. Naturally, first and foremost, they gained it from the Holy Scriptures. Added to this can be the apocryphal writings, liturgical and hagiographic texts as well as the sermons of the Church Fathers. As the sources were quite diverse a tremendous thematic richness was brought to the art.

Icons may be of monumental size for prominent display in churches or of a smaller scale for intimate devotion in the home. The most frequent subjects are Christ and the Mother of God.

What follows here is a sequence based more on the familiarity and recognisability of the subjects rather than a specific hierarchy.

The icon of **Christ** is the most familiar of all the icons probably because, in particular, it affirms the Incarnation. *(Plate 6)* The most common representation of Christ is of the Pantocrator - the Lord of the Universe. A large fresco of the Pantocrator is almost always to be found in the main dome of an Orthodox church. Iconographic canons dictate that the Pantocrator be depicted either in half-length or seated "in Majesty". In earlier representations the Christ figure had a rather stern look. After the iconoclastic period an evolution in the representation of Christ took place and, between the 14th and 16th centuries, in particular, the face of Christ becomes less stern and much warmer in appearance. It led to a greater balance between His human and Divine natures. The halo surrounding the head of Christ contains a cross inscribed with the Greek lettering

OϖN which means "I am who I am". The Christ figure wears a dark blue cloak which covers a red robe called a "*chiton*". The dark blue and red are regarded as royal colours and serve to remind us of His two distinct natures.

The next most visible and popular icon after the Christ is the icon of the **Mother of God**. *(Plate 7)* She is known as "*Theotokos*" which means "The Bearer of God". Orthodox tradition actually attributes the first icon of the Mother of God to St Luke the Evangelist who is said to have painted three of them soon after Pentecost. Icons of the Mother of God always show her with her hair and shoulders covered by a gold-bordered veil. This veil is called the "*maphirion*". Three golden stars are present on the veil; they are symbolic of her virginity before, during and after childbirth. The main iconographic representations of the Mother of God are the "*Theotokos*" Enthroned, The Mother Praying *(Orans),* the "*Hodigitria*" and the "*Eleousa*". In icons where the Virgin is holding the Christ-child, we see that the face of the child is that of an adult. The large forehead suggests eternal wisdom. The scroll the child holds contains the scriptures.

Besides the icons of Christ and the Virgin with Child which are so loved and admired by iconographers as well as the Orthodox faithful, there exists a host of other iconic subjects. The icon of **John the Baptist** is a familiar subject in iconography. St John is known as the Precursor or Forerunner.

Earlier, mention was made of the **Deësis** which appears on the iconostasis. There is also a Deësis icon. This smaller iconic version of the Deësis depicts only the Mother of God and St John the Baptist standing on either side of Christ.

The icon of the **Crucifixion** is always represented with the cross occupying the centre of the composition. The body of Christ is always elongated. It is gracefully portrayed and leans slightly towards his mother. As we look at the icon Mary stands on the left-

hand side often accompanied by other mourning women - including Mary Magdalena. On the right-hand side is his disciple, John, as well as the Roman centurion Longinus. At the foot of the cross there is a dark cave with the skull of Adam. The blood from Christ's wounds drip onto the skull in order to cleanse Adam of his sins thus enabling him to re-inherit eternal life.
The numerous other subjects depicted in icons are connected with the great feasts of the Orthodox church. There are ***twelve Great Feasts*** which create a theme around the greatest of all the feasts which is the **Resurrection of Christ**. This feast is represented by the icon titled the Resurrection of Christ, or the Descent into Hades.

The twelve Great Feasts are as follows:

1. The Nativity of the Mother of God.
2. The Presentation of Mary at the Temple.
3. The Annunciation.
4. The Dormition of the Mother of God.
5. The Nativity of Christ.
6. The Presentation of Jesus at the Temple.
7. The Baptism of Jesus.
8. The Transfiguration.
9. The Entry into Jerusalem.
10. The Ascension.
11. Pentecost.
12. The Exaltation of the Cross.

In addition to the Great Feasts there are a number of other feast which have their own icons.

To conclude this chapter it may be appropriate to refer to some of the other iconographic subjects with which, in the course of time, one should become familiar. These will often be represented in books or articles on the subject of icons and are usually referred to because they either represent outstanding examples of the art or, because they have a special significance within Orthodox or iconographic tradition.

A subject that is well-known and popular is that of **St Nicholas.** *(Plate 8*) He is occasionally portrayed in the form of a shoulder-length study, but most often he is depicted full-length. There is also a version of St Nicholas with "Scenes from his Life". This consists of St Nicholas occupying the central part of the panel which then has a border depicting his life from birth to death. St Nicholas was a bishop at Myra in Lycia and is believed to have been present at the First Ecumenical Council in Nicaea. After the Virgin Mary, he is by far the most popular subject of all the Saints painted by various iconographers. Other popular saints in iconography are **St Michael** and **St George**.

The icon of the **"Sinai Christ"** goes right back to 600 AD. *(Plate 9*) It is the earliest-known painted icon of Christ and contains all of the familiar features in its composition that we find in later versions of the Pantocrator. The technique of painting the hair and the beard are almost identical to later versions, as are the presence of the book and the way the right hand is held in a "blessing" position. The main elements of this icon are derived from Hellenistic and Egyptian traditions which, as we know, were the foundations for the early Christian icons. The icon is painted in wax encaustic which employs a process involving the "burning in" of colours by inlaying clays and baking or fusing the wax colours to the surface.

The icon of the **Virgin of Tenderness of Vladimir** is a variant of the Virgin *Eleousa* which assumed its final form in Byzantine art during the 11th century. According to tradition the "Vladimir" icon was painted by St Luke the Evangelist. It was brought from

Constantinople to Russia in the 12th century and installed in Vyshgorod near Kiev. In 1155 Prince Andrei Bogoliubskii transferred it to Vladimir, and installed it in the Cathedral of the Dormition where it was consecrated and given the additional name of "*Vladimirskaia*". It is a popular and much loved representation of the Virgin Mother and it later became the foremost object of veneration in the Vladimir-Suzdal region as well as in the rest of Muscovite Russia.

The icon of Andrei Rublev's **Holy Trinity** demands special mention. *(Plate 10)* From early times Christian iconography had unsuccessfully attempted to represent the Holy Trinity. The Byzantine model was known as the "*Philoxenia*" or the Hospitality of Abraham. As early as the 4th century this theme had been depicted in a mosaic which had shown Abraham receiving three visitors at the oak of Mamre. Recognising them as embodiments of the Trinity, he offers them hospitality bringing them water, bread and meat. The details of the earliest interpretations were historical rather than theological and, although the existence of the Trinity had been acknowledged at the Second Ecumenical Council in 381 AD, its precise nature had remained a constant source of controversy within Orthodoxy. It was not, however, until 1422 when the Holy monk and iconographer, Andrei Rublev, completed his icon of the subject that the perfect version was regarded as having been achieved. His version is said to correspond most fully to the church's teaching on the subject. Without diverting from the historical aspect of the event, Rublev, it is said, reduced the subject to a minimum so that the significance of the composition was to be found not in the *historical* biblical event that it depicted, but in its *dogmatic* meaning. With Rublev's version it became evident that the approach to treating this theme had been radically changed and in 1551 a council of the Russian Church declared that his Holy Trinity had been *"proto-revealed"*; meaning that it is a symbolic image inspired by God Himself. Rublev's Trinity is regarded as being the greatest of iconographic works and remains to this day as a classic example of the iconography of the Holy Trinity.

Lastly, it will be appropriate to mention the **Acheiropoietos** icon; which means "made without human hands". This image is an iconographical *type* rather than a specific extant example of an icon. The Tradition of the Orthodox Church declares that this image of the "Holy Face" is the first icon of Christ and one which appeared during His life on earth. According to legend this image of the Saviour reproduces the true appearance of Christ that had been impressed upon a cloth known as the *"mandylion"*. Christ, Himself, is alleged to have presented this cloth to King Abgar V of Edessa who was gravely ill and who had asked Christ to come to him. This image is regarded as the very first icon and serves as the source and basis for all the other images of Christ.

5

FAMOUS ICONOGRAPHERS

It is not easy to write about iconographers as they are quite difficult to identify! Traditionally they did not sign their work, so many recognisable works which we might see in museums, galleries or illustrated books will often simply be labelled as *"An unknown artist working at Chilandari", "Probably a Greek artist working at Ohrid"* or *"An unknown Serbian painter"*. It is only those iconographers who became known during their lifetimes, together with those who did actually sign their works, that we are able to identify with any degree of certainty.

It is especially during the era of the "post-Byzantine" schools in Crete that we begin to identify a significant number of iconographers mainly because of the fact that they were organised into guilds and became better known to the public. A number of iconographers began to sign their works and we become familiar with the names of well-known iconographers such as Andreas and Nicholas Ritzos, as well as Nicholas Tzafuris.

There are certain artists though, who have found a very special place in the iconographers' *"pantheon"*. They are Andrei Rublev, Dionysius, Theophanes the Greek; and with the iconographic renewal of the twentieth century, Fr. Gregory Kroug and Leonid Ouspensky.

Theophanes the Greek

Early in the 15th century an iconographer from Constantinople enjoyed considerable fame in Russia. He was known as

Theophanes the Greek. He began his career in Constantinople and the Crimea, but worked in Russia from about 1370 onwards. He produced large numbers of frescoes and wall paintings for churches and palaces. His great works include the frescoes of the Church of the Transfiguration in Novgorod, where he first achieved fame. After Novgorod he moved to Moscow where he produced the remarkable icon of the Deësis dedicated to the Cathedral of the Annunciation in the Kremlin. His style is regarded as innovative and individualistic and, his work is characterised by vigorous brushstrokes and unusual colours.

Andrei Rublev

Andrei Rublev is regarded as the greatest Russian painter. Not much is known about his life except that he was a monk in the monastery of Troitsky-Sergieva, and later, the monastery of Andronikov. He carried out large-scale works in collaboration with other artists and records suggest that he worked with Theophanes in the decoration of the iconostasis of the Cathedral of the Annunciation in Moscow. He also worked on the frescoes and icons in the Cathedral of the Dormition at Vladimir. Rublev's work is regarded as marking the birth of Russian classicism. His style is characterised by deep, pure colours, flowing curved lines, gentle expressions and, most of all, a feeling of intense spirituality. At the monastery at Zagorsk he painted the "Trinity" which is regarded as his masterpiece of iconography. In this icon he employed the "*scumbling*" technique for which he became renowned. This is the softening of the colours by applying thin coats of opaque colour. It gives the garments the impression of being of a transparent material. His work is considered to have been executed in the first truly

Russian style, exhibiting an adaptation of the more angular Byzantine style of painting.

Dionysius

Master Dionysii (Dionysius) was thought to have been born in the 1440s. Towards the end of the 15th century he was the director of a school in Moscow. During the late 1400s he carried out important painting commissions in the Cathedral of the Assumption in the Moscow Kremlin. In the late 1490s an artel - or artists' co-operative - headed by Dionysius painted the icons and the interiors of the Cathedral of the Assumption in the monastery of St Joseph of Volokolamsk. In the last years of his life he quite often worked in the area of Lake Belove where he painted the icons for the Pavlov-Obnorsky Monastery. Although Dionysius made use of the Byzantine prototype, his compositional treatment produced work that was distinctly Russian. His work is regarded as the most important phenomenon after Andrei Rublev in the history of Russian iconography.

After the decline of iconography in the 17th century we find ourselves having to wait until the iconic revival of the twentieth century to come across iconographers of any real substance. Alongside the work of Photius Kontoglou who is credited with having initiated the revival of the Byzantine tradition in his native Greece; the works of Leonid Ouspensky and Monk Gregory Kroug give testimony to the high levels of iconographic excellence that can be achieved when the theology and the art of the icon are rediscovered by people of deep faith.

Leonid Ouspensky

Leonid Ouspensky is regarded as one of the greatest contemporary masters of iconography. He was born in 1902 into a peasant family in Golosnovka in Russia. When he was twenty-five he moved to Paris where he devoted his entire life to iconography which he passionately loved. He never for one moment considered it simply a craft or a technique. He studied its early foundations and evolution, and besides teaching the art of iconography to students from all over the world he also became well-known for the remarkable theological treatises and books that he wrote. He died in 1987.

Gregory Kroug

Gregory Kroug was also born in Russia, in 1909, as George Kroug. After the revolution he emigrated to Estonia; thereafter moving to Paris where he studied at the Academy of Art. He remained in France for the rest of his life. His icons look different from the style of icon with which we might have become familiar. They look almost "modern" - to give them a label. Each one, however, is regarded as a unique masterpiece. He painted in excess of five hundred different panels in the course of his life. Many of them have not lasted very long because of the inferior quality of the materials with which he had to work. They have also suffered from pollution damage as well as, sadly, general neglect.

The Lebanese painter and writer, Mahmoud Zibawi, best sums up Gregory Kroug's legacy when he says, "*....the work of Gregory Kroug shows a burst of spiritual splendour that characterised the art of earlier times. From the beautiful icons of the Church of Saint-Seraphim at Montgeron to the daring frescoes of the Hermitage of the Holy Spirit at Mesnil - Saint-Denis, Father Gregory Kroug* *magisterially affirms his gifts as a painter dedicated to Orthodoxy. The great synthesis realised by the great painters of living forms of the past is here illuminated by the living breath of genius, proper to the iconographer".*[3]

Father Gregory remained a simple monk for the rest of his days living an ascetic life up to the time of his death, in Paris, in 1969.

---

[3] Zibawi, M: *The Icon: Its Meaning and History*: Page 151

6

HOW ARE ICONS PAINTED?

The most traditional method of painting an icon is the use of egg tempera on a gesso-covered wooden panel. Although new materials appear from time to time, the traditional methods and techniques going right back to antiquity are the ones still used, almost without change, by contemporary iconographers.

First, a non-resinous wooden panel is selected and prepared. The initial preparation involves the covering of the panel with layers of gesso. The gesso is the link between the wood and the paint and it requires patience and expertise to ensure that the perfect surface is created on which to paint. The gesso is painted on in liquid form. It consists of alabaster powder or chalk mixed with gelatine. It is painted on with each succeeding layer being thinner than the previous one. This prevents cracking. When all the gesso layers have been applied the panel is left to dry and then sanded to give a smooth finish. Once the panel has been prepared in this way the outline of the image to be painted is traced onto it. This outline is then scratched or incised into the gesso by using a sharp tool such as an awl. This incision helps the iconographer to follow the shape of the composition once the panel has been flooded with the first layers of pigment.

If gilding is to be done, it is done at this point before the painting begins in order to prevent the gold from sticking to the pigment. After the gilding, the actual painting begins. The icon is painted with egg tempera which is a mixture of egg yolk, water and coloured pigments which are in the form of fine powders.

The painting proceeds by definite consecutive stages. Briefly, these can be listed as follows:

- painting the background colours
- redrawing the outlines or incisions that were made
- building up the layers of lights
- the highlighting and finishing process

The building up of the layers of lights refers to the technique of applying the various colours starting with the darker colours and gradually making them lighter as each new layer is painted. This is done not only on the figures and the landscapes, but especially on the faces and other uncovered parts of the body. The faces and the hands are considered to be the most important parts of the icon. The face gives the icon its theological meaning whilst the hand gestures dictate the manner in which the clothing moves and folds. Adding the final layers of lights to the face requires exceptional consideration and care as they will contribute to the spiritual feeling of the face. The iconographer will bring all his expertise to bear on this process so that the prototype is captured as exactly as possible.

In completing his work the iconographer checks all the details. The eyes and the lips are carefully defined as the expression depends on these. The final highlights are then placed in certain positions on the face such as above and under the eyes, on the tip of the nose as well as on the forehead, earlobe and chin. The time has now come to add the lettering or the inscription. This final act is what turns the work into an icon. It is by the inscription that the icon achieves its spiritual dimension, its sacred character and its presence. The lettering is always done in one of the languages of the Byzantine liturgy such as Greek or Slavonic. Icons of Christ bear the abbreviated inscription "IC XC" whilst Mother of God icons have "MP OY". *(Diagram 6)* The inscription is not a title; it serves as a communion with the bearer of the name. Egon Sendler says, "*Through the inscription, the icon is linked to its prototype, the person represented in it. Along with this person, the icon participates in the heavenly liturgy and makes this celebration present in our midst*".[4]

Icons are never framed like other pictures; instead, at the time that the inscriptions are done, a red "frame" is usually painted around the border of the icon. This serves to provide a "separation" between the holy image and the mundane world. Sometimes an icon has an ornate metal covering. This is called the "riza" or "oklad". The idea of the oklad was first introduced in the sixteenth century. Its function is purely decorative. *(Plate 11)*

A point worth making is that an iconographer should not sign his work. There are a number of reasons for this, the most significant of which could be the fact that the icon is painted according to tradition as well as from documentation which is not in actual fact the artist's property. In addition, it can be said that the "inspiration" for what the artist has done has come not from himself, but from the Holy Spirit. It is for this reason that an icon is usually described as having been "*painted from*" a particular prototype "*by the hand of*" the iconographer.

In conclusion, it should be mentioned that when painting from a particular prototype, an iconographer never attempts to replicate any of the damaged sections. This is tantamount to attempting to "fake" the icon. In the course of time many of the beautiful old prototypes from which the iconographer is painting will have been damaged. They may have missing sections, cracks, or paint which is peeling off. It may, therefore, be very difficult to know exactly how the original icon looked. The iconographer will, therefore, need to study reproductions, or other prototypes from the same period and school

---

[4] Sendler, E: *The Icon: Image of the Invisible*: Page 215

in order to make the necessary comparisons so that the icon he is painting is as close as possible to the prototype in its original form. Remember that, theoretically, there is no such thing as a "fake" icon. As already pointed out icons are not copied; they are *"painted from"* the prototype. If an icon is painted according to iconographic canon and Church Tradition it is an authentic icon. It becomes a "fake" only if it is artificially made to look old in order to falsify its date of origin.

7

LIVING WITH ICONS

Although its origins go back hundreds of years, there is presently a return to the icon as much from the spiritual as from the artistic point of view. Some people regard the icon as representing a preciously sacred inheritance from centuries ago, whereas for others it has quite simply become an object of sublime beauty.

By now it will have become clear that the icon plays an especially important role in Orthodox Christianity. Orthodoxy is one of the great branches of Christianity and has been described as being close to Roman Catholicism in doctrine, but close to Protestantism in feeling. All three of these branches of Christianity live in close communion with each other on the basis of the same values as well as subscribing to the same theology. It is for this reason that the icon can find a place in all of these Christian traditions. The Roman Catholic Church, for example, confesses, as does Orthodoxy, the dogma of the veneration of icons; and although icons do not have a liturgical or sacramental role in Protestantism, they do have a certain dynamic which strikes a chord with many Protestants insofar they serve as an effective vehicle for the Christian message. Icons, therefore, are often present in Roman Catholic as well as Protestant churches as items of decoration. Some, in fact, can be seen adorning the walls of Winchester Cathedral as well as Westminster Abbey in London.

Visiting Churches

One of the most familiar sights you will see when travelling through Orthodox lands, particularly Greece, is the domed Byzantine-style churches which punctuate the landscape. *(Plate 12)* Don't pass them by. Go inside; they are rarely locked. If, on the other hand, the church *is* locked, the house of the priest, or a caretaker will usually be nearby, and your polite request to see inside will almost always gladly be agreed to.

Whoever has opened the church for you will not expect a tip but do feel free to light a candle and place a donation in the box provided. Once inside, you will have the opportunity to experience *in situ* much of what we have talked about in the book. You will surely be fascinated by what you see. A wonderful atmosphere is created by the smell of incense as well as by the richness of all the gold glowing in the light created by the candles, sanctuary lamps and sunlight filtering through the windows.

Attending a Liturgy

Having visited an Orthodox church in order to look at the icons and the frescoes you might now find it interesting to attend a Divine Liturgy. This may sound like an intimidating suggestion but it isn't really. Simply go along and ensconce yourself on the periphery of proceedings where you can get a good view of what is going on. Take along some money in case a collection is taken or if you want to light a candle. One of the highlights of the service is the beautiful *a cappella* Byzantine chanting. The services can be long, so feel free to leave once you feel you have seen and heard enough. This is the way things are done. A homely atmosphere prevails with worshippers coming and going throughout the service.

There is a story of Prince Vladimir of Kiev sending his ambassadors to foreign lands to compare different religions in order to assist him in his "choice of faith" for his principality. After having been

present at a Divine Liturgy in the magnificent Hagia Sophia in Constantinople, they returned home to report to their Prince:
"We knew not whether we were in heaven or on earth, for assuredly on earth such beauty cannot be found anywhere else. So we do not know what we ought to tell you; but one thing we know well: God dwells among those men who celebrate His glory in such a manner that no other religion on this earth could equal. It is impossible for us to forget such splendorous beauty".

Attending a service in an Orthodox church will give you a glimpse of what they meant. You will be captivated by it all!

Museums, Galleries and Bookshops

In order to gain a further understanding and appreciation of icons it is a good idea to visit museums and galleries. Also, a visit to art showrooms can be beneficial. In art showrooms, especially, the owners will be more than happy to respond to any queries. Having chosen to exhibit and sell icons it should be assumed that they are quite knowledgeable on the subject. You will also have the opportunity to view and appreciate them at very close range. This will enable you to pick up on some of the finer points of the composition. Another good opportunity to see a cross-section of icons is by visiting auction rooms to view them before they "go under the hammer".
You may also derive tremendous pleasure from paging through beautiful "coffee table-style" illustrated books on the subject of icons. As icons become more popular, so more of these types of books are appearing. If you are thinking of building up a collection of books on icons you will enjoy browsing through them in bookshops. The sorts of bookshops to look for are art bookshops

as well as specialist bookshops with publications about Greece, the Balkans and other eastern European countries. Incidentally, specialist bookshops often also sell CDs or cassettes of eastern Orthodox music. Similar music is, of course, available in the Classical section of music shops. It can be both relaxing and uplifting to listen to this type of music - especially so as background music whilst painting icons!

Acquiring your own Icon

What about acquiring your own icon? As you begin to know them better you may soon decide upon a particular subject that is your favourite. You may wish to own one of these to adorn your home. How do you go about it ?

First a word of caution. Be mindful of the kind of "touristy" icons that are often available in souvenir shops. When travelling in Orthodox lands you will often come across these "icons" which purport to be the authentic, handpainted thing. They are often styled as "handpainted" or "handmade". In some instances the original image *has* been painted by hand but it has then been machine-transferred onto a block and many identical factory-produced panels have been churned out. They are not, therefore, as you may believe all individually handpainted panels. But, if this is all that you really want - a simple, reasonably priced reproduction - good and well; the important thing is to be aware of what you are buying. Many carry a so-called "certificate of authenticity". Examine the wording closely as it can often be quite ambiguous.

The best route for acquiring an authentic icon is from a reputable icon dealer or by commissioning an iconographer to paint one for you. If you take the latter course you have a good chance of acquiring exactly what you want and at the price you can afford. If you decide to buy an icon from a gallery that deals in icons, you will be well advised first to visit a few to see what is available. You will have an opportunity to discuss with the gallery owner what you want and, at the same time, be able to find out about the "pedigree" of any icon you have in mind to buy. You will also learn about the things that affect the price of the icon such as age, quality, country of origin or school - and even the iconographer, if this is known.

Painting an Icon

Having acquired a fairly broad knowledge of icons, you may now even be keen to attempt to paint them. The Orthodox church believes that icon painters should be good artists as well as sincere Christians. Provided that you have a reasonable talent, patience and a genuine desire to do it properly and, in the appropriate spirit, there is no reason why you should not learn to paint them as well. Start off by reading up on the technique of icon painting in books or painting manuals. It is difficult to teach yourself this art form, so if you decide to pursue it you are best advised to find a master iconographer to tutor you. Once found, a tutor will advise you exactly as to the materials you will need. Do not buy anything before this time.

Possibly the most important thing to be borne in mind before embarking upon this venture is to remember that it can be a costly and time-consuming undertaking. You must ensure that you have a suitable location in which to work as well as the time to pursue the activity. Once you're under way though, you will soon realise how rewarding and spiritually uplifting it is.

8

SOME FINAL THOUGHTS

The icon is currently finding its way into Western culture at an unprecedented pace. With the dramatic changes that have taken place in eastern Europe in the 1990s icons are being brought from eastern Orthodox countries in significant numbers and are now to be found in museums and art galleries around the world. As a work of art in its own right, it is not unusual nowadays to find beautiful icons hanging side by side with Van Goghs or Picassos in private collections.

The icon attracts believers and non-believers alike and generates various degrees of interest in those who want to learn more about it. Above all, however, there is the religious attraction - a desire to understand the icon and through it to come closer to understanding Orthodoxy, the Incarnation and, Christianity itself. For, after all, the icon exists to affirm the Incarnation, and it is the Incarnation that is the cornerstone of Christianity.

There is really no reason, therefore, for any Christian home to be without an icon. All Orthodox Christians display an icon on a wall or in a "prayer corner" in their homes. In a world where we are often inclined to retain our church affiliations without readily practising our Christianity, the presence of an icon in our homes can serve subconsciously to remind us of our faith. It can be very calming to sit in a room where an icon is present and to gaze upon it. We might appreciate it purely for its intrinsic artistic beauty; but above all, it may in many instances, act as a catalyst to silent contemplation or prayer.

Maps

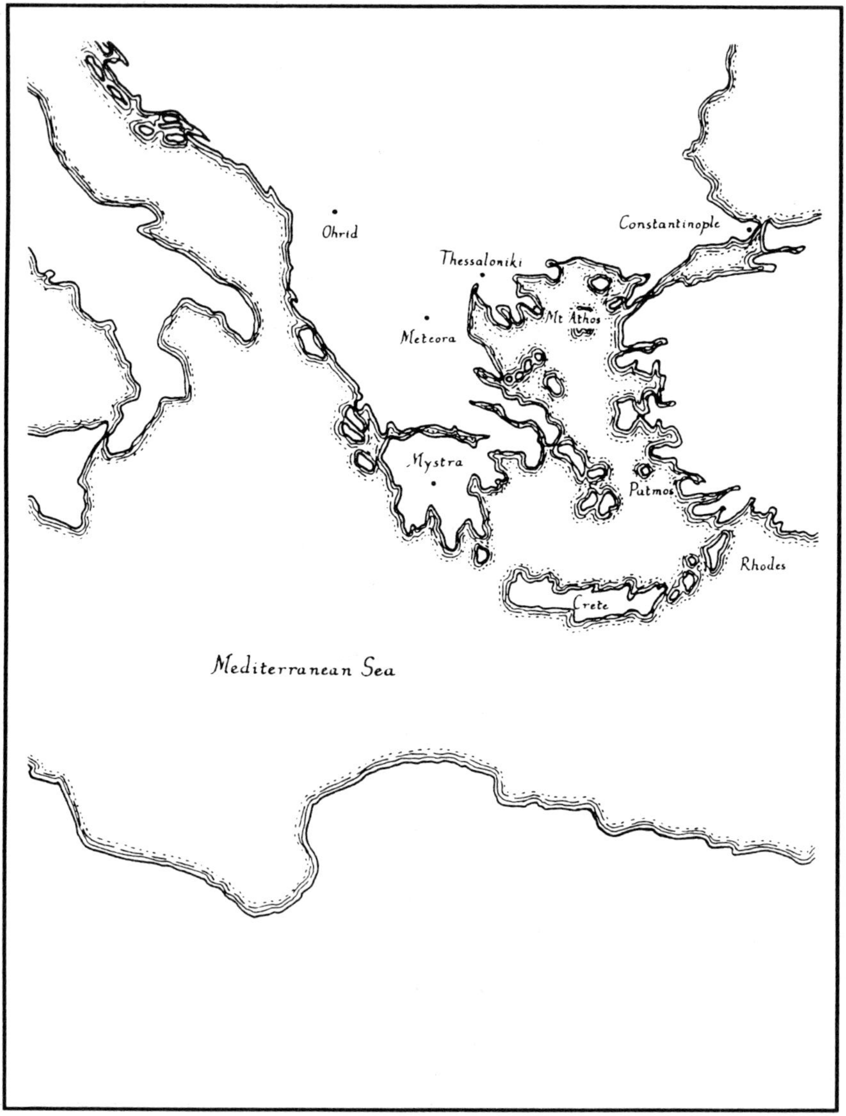

Map 1. Places mentioned in the text: Greece and the Balkans

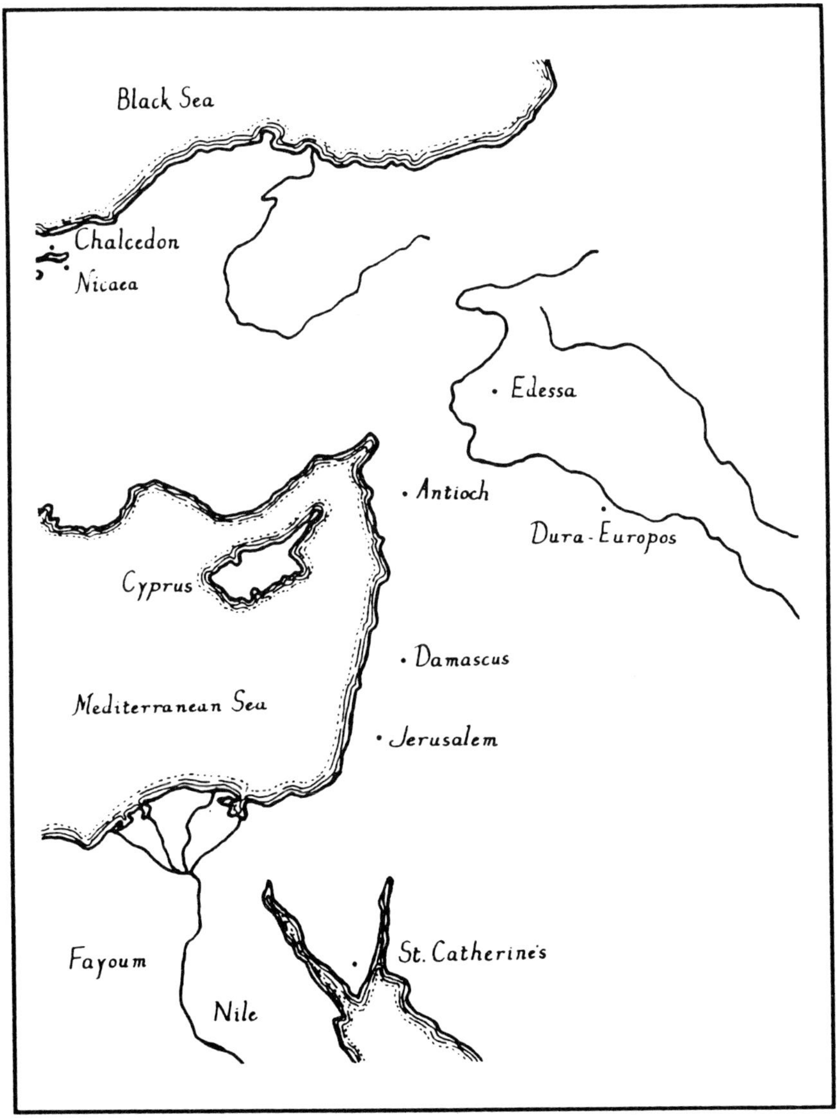

Map 2. Places mentioned in the text: Eastern Mediterranean

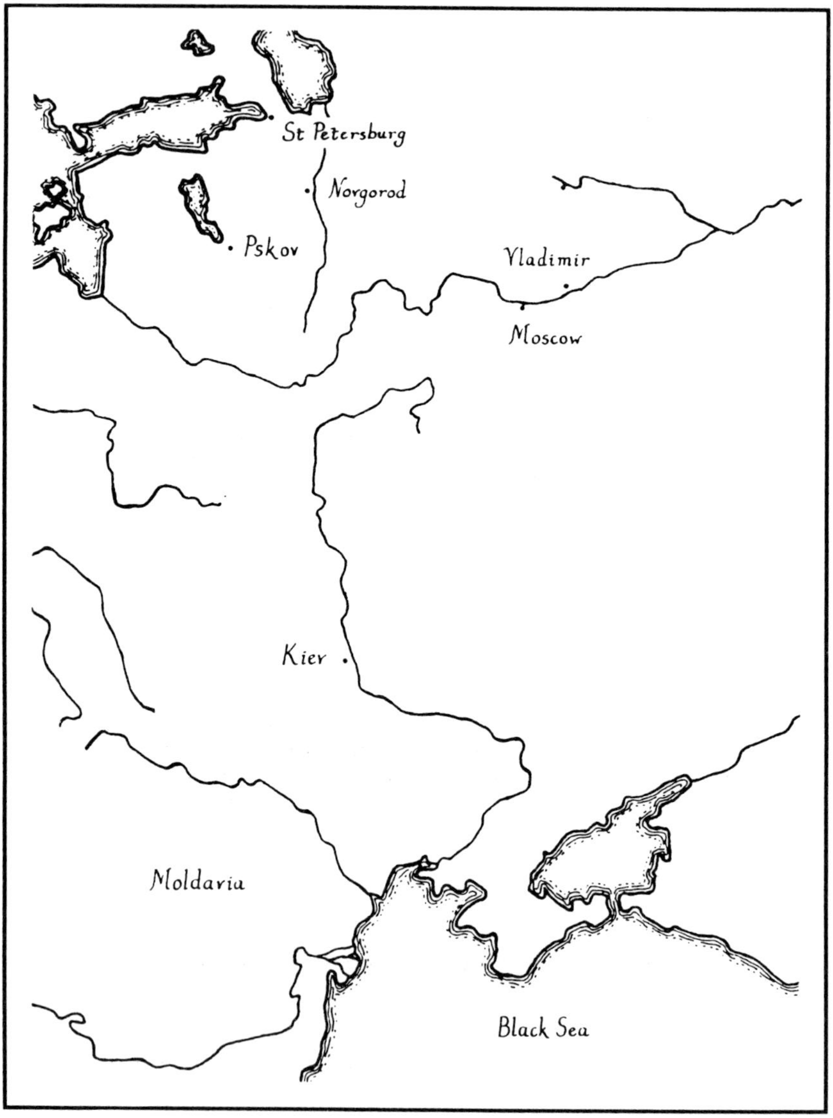

Map 3. Places mentioned in the text: Russia

GLOSSARY

a cappella:
Singing without instrumental accompaniment.

Acheiropoietos:
"Not made by human hands". This name is usually given to icons ascribed to supernatural intervention.

Annunciation:
The announcement of the Incarnation by the angel Gabriel to the Virgin Mary. (Luke 1: 26-38)

Apocrypha:
The fourteen books included as an appendix to the Old Testament in the Septuagint and the Vulgate but not included in the Hebrew canon. They are not printed in the Protestant versions of the Bible. Apocryphal literature is an important source of details of the life of the Virgin Mary.

Archiepiscopal:
Associated with an archbishop.

Ascension:
The final passing of Jesus Christ from earth into heaven. (Acts 1:9-12)

Byzantine Empire:
A continuation of the Roman Empire in the eastern Mediterranean centred on what is now Istanbul in Turkey. Established in the fourth century AD, it survived in various shapes and sizes until its invasion and fall at the hands of the Ottoman Turks in 1453.

Canon:
A church decree enacted to regulate religious practices.

Catacombs:
An underground burial place consisting of tunnels with vaults leading off them for tombs.

Coptic:
Of the Copts. A native Egyptian Christian. A member of an independent sect of the Eastern Church.

Cosmic:
Of or relating to the whole universe.

De-materialise:
To cease to have a material existence, i.e. to become spiritual.

Diocese:
A district under the jurisdiction of a bishop.

Discourse:
A formal treatment of a subject in speech or writing; to hold a discussion.

Doctrine:
A body of teachings of a religious group.

Dogma:
A religious system of beliefs proclaimed by church authority as true.

Dormition:
The taking up of the Virgin Mary (body and soul) into heaven when her earthly life was ended. Early apocryphal literature contains several versions of the story of the "death" of the Virgin. Some of these date from the 4th century. The *Golden Legend* which appeared in the 13th century gives an extended account of this story based on the apocryphal works.

Ecumenical (council):
An assembly of bishops and other ecclesiastic representatives of the Christian Church throughout the world.

Egg-tempera:
A mixture of egg-yolk, water and coloured pigments used in painting.

Eleousa:
"Mercy" or "Tenderness". An iconographic representation of the Mother of God.

Eucharist:
The Christian sacrament in which Christ's Last Supper is commemorated by the consecration of bread and wine, i.e. the taking of communion.

Evangelist:
Any of the writers of the New Testament Gospels, i.e. Mathew, Mark, Luke or John.

Excommunicate:
To exclude a person from the communion of believers and from the privileges and public prayers of the church.

Frescoes:
Wallpaintings using watercolours on wet plaster.

Frontality:
A view from the front.

Hagiography:
The writings of the lives of the Saints.

Hellenistic:
Characteristic of the principles, ideals and pursuits associated with Greek civilisation (c323-30 BC).

Heresies:
An opinion contrary to the official doctrine of the Christian Church.

Hodigitria:
"She who shows the way" - the name by which a prototype of the Virgin Mary is known. In the "Hodigitria" composition the Mother of God points to the Christ Child whilst holding Him with her left arm. From the 9th century it became the Byzantine icon *par excellence;* and one to which the Byzantine emperors were accustomed to pray to for "guidance" when they went into battle.

Hypostasis:
The *one* person of Christ in which the divine and human natures are united.

Iconoclast:
A destroyer of religious images or sacred objects.

Iconodule:
A person who supports the veneration of icons in worship.

Incarnation:
The assuming of a *human body* by the Son of God.

Liturgy (Divine):
The form of public services officially prescribed by a church. Within the eastern Orthodox Churches the Divine Liturgy refers to the order of service laid down for the celebration of the Eucharist.

Metropolitan:
Within the eastern Orthodox church, it is the head of an ecclesiastical province, ranking between archbishop and patriarch.

Mother of God:
The Virgin Mary.

Mount Athos:
A peninsula in northern Greece jutting out into the Aegean from Halkidiki. It is the principal centre of monasticism for the Orthodox Church. It functions as an autonomous republic within the state of Greece.

Narthex:
A rectangular entrance hall between the porch and the nave of a church.

Nativity:
The birth of Jesus Christ. (Matthew 2:1-12, Luke 2:1-20)

Nave:
The central part of the church.

Orans:
"Praying" - a title given to the Virgin when she is depicted in a standing position with her arms outstretched, praying.

Orthodoxy:
Conforming to the Christian Faith as established by the early church. The Orthodox Church is the Eastern church which separated from theWestern church in the 9th century, recognising the Patriarch of Constantinople as its head. Orthodox lands include Greece, Russia, and the Balkan countries.

Palaeologan (period):
The Palaeologan dynasty ruled from 1261 to the fall of the Byzantine Empire in 1453. There was a great intellectual and artistic flowering during this period.

Pantocrator:
Lord of the Universe or Christ in Triumph. In Byzantine art it applied specifically to the half-length or enthroned representations of Christ situated in the domes of churches - and, of course, depicted as the subject of icons.

Patriarch:
Within the Orthodox Church, the bishops of the four ancient principal sees of Constantinople. Antioch, Alexandria and Jerusalem as well as the chief bishops of Russia, Romania and Serbia.

Pentecost:
A Christian festival occurring on Whit Sunday commemorating the descent of the Holy Spirit on the apostles. (Acts 2:1-4)

Perspective:
The theory of art whereby three-dimensional objects are depicted on a two-dimensional surface. The objects are drawn as getting smaller as they recede into the background. The vanishing point is away from the viewer.

Profile:
A *side* view of an object - especially a face or head.

Prototype:
Something that serves as an example of a type.

Refractions:
Deflections. The change in direction of light.

Renaissance:
The period of European history marking the end of the Middle Ages and the rise of the Modern World, usually considered as beginning in Italy in the 14th century.

Sacrament:
An outward sign combined with a prescribed form of words and regarded as conferring some special grace upon those who receive it.

Sanctuary:
The part of a church building in which the main altar stands.

Schools (of iconography):
A group of iconographers linked by the same style.

Theology:
The systematic study of Christian revelation concerning God's nature and purpose.

Theotokos:
"The Bearer of God"- one of the titles of the Virgin.

Tradition:
Within Orthodoxy, Tradition refers to the living continuity of all aspects of the *Faith.* Timothy Ware sums it up succinctly when he says, "Tradition means the books of the Bible; it means the Creed; it means the decrees of the Ecumenical Councils and the Writings of the Fathers; it means the Canons, the Service Books, the Holy Icons - in fact, the whole system of doctrine, Church government, worship, spirituality and art which Orthodoxy has articulated over the ages".

Transfiguration:
The change in the appearance of Christ that took place before three of His disciples - Peter, James and John - when Christ manifested His Divine nature to them. He took them up a mountain - traditionally Mount Tabor in Galilee - and in their presence His change in appearance took place; His face shone like the sun and his clothes became dazzling white. Moses and Elijah appeared on either side of Him and spoke with Him. A bright cloud overshadowed them and a voice from heaven said, "This is my Son". The Apostles fell prostrate before the vision. (Matthew 17:1-13, Mark 9:2-13, Luke 9:28-36).

Treatise:
A formal work on a subject.

Two-dimensional:
Having two dimensions - length and breadth, but no volume or depth.

Veneration:
To hold deep respect or reverence for something.

MUSEUMS AND MAJOR COLLECTIONS OF ICONS

Bulgaria:	The National Gallery, Sofia
Cyprus:	Byzantine Museum, Nicosia; St Neofytos Monastery, Paphos
Egypt:	St Catherine's Monastery, Mount Sinai
England:	The British Museum, London
Finland:	The National Museum, Helsinki
Former Yugoslavia:	Museum of the Orthodox Serbian Churches, Belgrade; Museum of Historical Monuments, Ohrid; The Art Gallery, Skopje
Germany:	Icon Museum, Recklinghausen
Greece:	Benaki Museum, Athens; Byzantine Museum, Athens; Convents at Meteora; Museums at Mistra; Historical Museum, Heraklion, Crete; Agia Aikaterini, Heraklion, Crete; Monastery of St John, Patmos; Metropolitan Palace, Rhodes; Monasteries on Mount Athos
Italy:	Hellenic Institute of Byzantine Art, Venice; Church of San Giorgio dei Greci, Venice

Israel:	The Great Orthodox Patriarchate, Jerusalem
Romania:	The Art Museum, Bucharest
Russia:	Tretiakov Gallery, Moscow; Andrei Rublev Museum, Moscow; Cathedrals of the Kremlin, Moscow; The Hermitage, St Petersburg; Russian National Museum, St Petersburg; Novgorod Museum, Novgorod; Cathedral of the Trinity, Zagorsk
Turkey:	Ecumenical Patriarchate, Constantinople (Istanbul)
United States of America:	Dumbarton Oaks Collection, Washington

SELECT BIBLIOGRAPHY

Babic, Gordana: *Icons* (Bracken Books, London, 1988)
Bulkin, Valentin: *Dionysius* (St Petersburg, Aurora Art Publishers, 1982)
Dionysius of Fourna: *The Painter's Manual* (Hetherington, P. trans.) (Oakwood Publications, 1989)
Evdokimov, Paul: *The Art of the Icon: A Theology of Beauty* (Anthony Clarke Publications, Wheathampstead, 1990)
Frangopoulos, Athanasios: *Our Orthodox Christian Faith* (Brotherhood of Theologians, Athens, 1974)
Gage, Nicholas: *Hellas: A Portrait of Greece* (Efstathiadis Group S.A., Attikis, 1993)
Grierson, Roderick (Ed): *Gates of Mystery: The Art of Holy Russia* (Exhibition Catalogue) (InterCultura, Fort Worth, 1993)
Hall, John: *Hall's Dictionary of Subjects and Symbols in Art* (John Murray, London, 1991)
Lassus, Jean: *The Early Christian and Byzantine World* (Paul Hamlyn, London, 1967)
Limouris, Gennadios (Ed): *Icons: Windows on Eternity* (WCC Publications, Geneva, 1990)
Muzj, Maria Giovanna: *Transfiguration: Introduction to the Contemplation of Icons* (St Paul's Multimedia Productions, Slough, 1991)
Nichols O.P., Aidan: *The Art of God Incarnate: Theology and Image in Christian Tradition* (Darton, Longman and Todd, London, 1980)
Ouspensky, Leonid: *The Theology of the Icon,* Vol I and 11 (St Vladimir's Seminary Press, Crestwood, 1991)
Ouspensky, L and Lossky,V: *The Meaning of Icons* (St Vladimir's Seminary Press, 1982)
Papaioannou, Kostas: *Byzantine and Russian Painting* (Heros Books, London, 1968)
Quenot, Michel: *The Icon: Window on the Kingdom* (Mowbray, London, 1991)

Ramos-Poqui, Guillem: *The Technique of Icon Painting* (Search Press Ltd and Burns and Oats Ltd, Tunbridge Wells, 1990)
Runciman, Steven: *Byzantine Style and Civilization* (Penguin Books, London, 1975)
Sendler, Egon: *The Icon: Image of the Invisible* (Oakwood Publications, Torranance, CA, 1988)
Sophocleous, Sophocles: *Icons of Cyprus: 7th-20th Century* (Museum Publications, Nicosia, 1994)
Talbot Rice, David: *Art of the Byzantine Era* (Thames and Hudson Ltd, London, 1993)
Taylor, John: *Icon Painting* (Phaidon Press Ltd, Oxford, 1979)
Temple, Richard: *A Brief Illustrated History of Icons* (The Temple Gallery, London, 1992)
Temple, Richard: *Icons and the Origins of Christian Mysticism* (Element Books, Shaftesbury, 1990)
Tregubov, Andrew: *The Light of Christ: Iconography of Gregory Kroug* (St Vladimir's Seminary Press, Crestwood, 1990)
Ware, Timothy: *The Orthodox Church* (Penguin Books, London, 1993)
Weitzmann, Kurt; et al: *The Icon* (Evans Brothers, London, 1982)
Yanagi, Munemoto; et al: *Byzantium* (Cassell Ltd, London, 1978)
Zibawi, Mahmoud: *The Icon: Its Meaning and History* (The Liturgical Press, Collegeville, 1993)

“Icons are dynamic manifestations of man’s spiritual power to redeem creation through beauty and art.

The iconographers aimed at demonstrating that men, animals and plants, and the whole cosmos could be rescued from their present state of degradation and restored to their proper “image”.

The icons were pledges of the coming victory of a redeemed creation over the fallen one”

Nicholas Zernov

Other Titles available from Loizou Publications

Nikos G. Assiminios
Salvation or Death
ISBN 0 9521246 1 0

C.P. Cavafy
A Bilingual Collection of Poems
By C.P. Cavafy
Translated by Edmund Keeley and Philip Sherrard
ISBN 0 9521246 2 9
(An audio cassette of Cavafy's poetry is also available)

Alexandros Papadiamantis
The Murderess - I Phonissa
(A bilingual novel - Greek and English)
ISBN 0 9521246 0 2